PERSPECTIVES ON
ORGANIZATION THEORY

PERSPECTIVES ON
ORGANIZATION THEORY

ANNA GRANDORI

BALLINGER PUBLISHING COMPANY
Cambridge, Massachusetts
A Subsidiary of Harper & Row, Publishers, Inc.

International Standard Book Number: 0-88730-214-9

Library of Congress Catalog Card Number: 87-11359

Printed in the United States of America

Library of Congress Cataloging-in-Publication Data

Grandori, Anna.
  Perspectives on organization theory.

  Translation of: Teorie dell'organizzazione.
  Bibliography: p.
  Includes index.
  1. Organization. 2. Management. 3. Organizational behavior.
4. Organizational change. 5. Corporate planning. I. Title.
HD37.I8G7313   1987   302.3'5   87-11359
ISBN 0-88730-214-9

To my family

A.G.

"For within serious economic theory there are no such things as 'schools' or differences of principle. . . . There are differences in exposition, . . . in technique, . . . in individual pieces of the analytic machine, . . . [and] finally there are differences as to particular problems. But this is all."

J.A. Schumpeter
The Instability of Capitalism

CONTENTS

LIST OF FIGURES

LIST OF TABLES

FOREWORD

I first read (or tried to read) this book in the original Italian version. Professor Grandori and I exchanged books we had written when I arrived at Bocconi University in Milan as a visiting professor in January 1985. At first, I was casually trying to translate the book in order to improve my knowledge of the Italian language. As I got further into the reading, though, I became increasingly interested in the way the subject of organizations was treated. Uncertain whether I was simply projecting my own ideas into a language I was learning, I asked Giorgio Inzerilli, now at Erasmus University, to read parts of the book and to translate some specific sections for me. Inzerilli was, as I, impressed with Professor Grandori's analysis of organizational approaches.

Thus assured that I was not drastically mistranslating the ideas in the text, I recommended to Bill Roberts, then at Pitman (which was later sold to Ballinger), that he publish the book. Bill, knowing my fluency in Italian, asked to see some translated material. Professor Grandori sent him several translated chapters, which he asked Karl Weick to review. On the strength of that recommendation, Roberts agreed to publish the English translation.

Anyone with a serious interest in organizations will find *Perspectives on Organization Theory* very helpful. In it, Professor Grandori analyzes the fundamental structure underlying some current approaches to the study of organizations. She distills the essence of each of the approaches, showing conceptual overlaps and areas of divergence.

Professor Grandori's background as an economist serves her well in that she understands the external market of firms in economic terms. Further, as her analysis of Oliver Williamson's work demonstrates, it allows her to describe the underlying assumptions about markets implicit in these models and how these assumptions limit the applicability of the model.

Some readers will be disappointed because Professor Grandori did not subject their preferred approach to analysis and discussion. While the nature of the task she undertakes in this book creates inevitable gaps, her *approach* to the analysis is her invaluable contribution to the study of organizations. It would be useful to do more critical analysis of the type that she does so well here.

Henry L. Tosi

ACKNOWLEDGMENTS

This research has been supported by the Ministero Pubblica Istruzione (MPI), the Centro Nazionale della Ricerca (CNR), and the Cassa di Risparmio delle Province Lombarde.

I am grateful to Henry Tosi for his valuable guidance on the revised U.S. version of this book—for his help with content and style and for his always available sympathy. My thanks also go to the researchers in the United States who met with me during my visits to the United States, particularly Paul Lawrence, James March, Robert Miles, Jeffrey Pfeffer, and Gerald Salancik.

I also am indebted to my colleagues in the Department of Organizational Behavior at Bocconi University, with whom I have discussed and worked on the models presented in this book. I thank particularly Andrea Rugiadini, Raoul C.D. Nacamulli, Vincenzo Perrone, and Severino Salvemini for their help.

This book never would have been possible without the contributions of Crispian Piggott, who first translated the manuscript into English. He successfully became familiar not only with my ideas but also with the U.S. organizational theories discussed in this book.

I am solely responsible, of course, for the contents—and the limitations—of this book.

INTRODUCTION

Theories about organizations have proliferated during the 1970s and 1980s. This book provides a critical analysis of the state of the art and compares main current theories. It also presents some ideas on how to apply these theories to organizational design.

In recent years, the most important new organization theories have been analyses that focused on macro-organizational issues. These usually are applicable to business organizations but in some cases also apply to other kinds of institutions. The most innovative organizational research has tended to shift from organization of work in the classical sense (that is, job design and organization at the work-flow level) to explaining and designing the entire firm's organizational arrangement (such as the criteria that determine specialization and how to coordinate organizational units) and to interfirm organization. For this reason, too, this book focuses on macro-organizational issues.

The analysis centers largely on the debate that has been developing in the United States. Two important European schools are considered because of their influence on the U.S. debate—the University of Aston School in the United Kingdom and Michel Crozier's school in France. This is not, however, to deny the existence of other developments in Europe, especially because during the period covered in this book organizational thinking in Europe has been moving away from U.S. influence and independent institutions have been founded for the study of organizations.[1]

Major current perspectives on organizations, which are discussed here, seem to have developed in an apparently independent fashion and draw on different concepts and definitions. They often are thought to be ways of looking at organizations through different glasses or rival paradigms (Kuhn 1962). It is argued here that the main models differ mostly because they have different domains of application. Understanding where and how they differ or overlap allows us to select some of the conceptual tools they offer to improve our capacity to solve organizational problems.

Chapter 1 shows how these new perspectives on organizations share a common starting point—the theory of the organization as an information-processing system. Originally postulated in March and Simon's (1958) seminal work, it has been further developed by the authors of the structural contingencies theory (see Chapter 1) into prescriptive models applicable to the design of business organizations (Lawrence and Lorsch 1967; Thompson 1967; Galbraith 1973). This set of related theories was the dominant scientific paradigm in the field of the organizational theory of the firm during the 1960s and early 1970s.

The main new theories considered here instead should be viewed as different new research programs (Lakatos 1970)—sets of related studies aimed at solving different problems, among which connections are possible but not yet clear.[2] The main thesis advanced here concerning relationships among the new research programs is that, in the domains where they do not overlap—in the sense that they actually generate the same predictions provided an adequate translation between their theoretical languages—these approaches predict organizational behavior under different conditions and assumptions about the form and content of the firm's goals.

Each chapter of this book examines the set of organizational arrangements that a firm can adopt and through which process it can achieve its goals given specific assumptions about its preference function. The models first presented are based on the most restrictive conditions, under which there is no conflict among objectives and the expected consequences of alternative organizational structures can be assessed. Next, models with less restrictive conditions are discussed, concluding with those in which there is no *a priori* information about either the actors' preferences or the consequences of organizational actions.

The first research program is presented in Chapter 2 and is based on the hypothesis that the firm's preference function is a unique objective that is measurable in terms of profitability. Where interfirm and not internal organization is the problem, the preference ordering of different firms over different alternatives of interorganizational arrangement is assumed to be homogeneous.[3] This research program is known as the markets and hierarchies approach (M&H) (Williamson and Ouchi 1981). It has been developed around a core model, the organizational failures framework (OFF), postulated by Oliver Williamson (1975), that makes use of the approach and concepts of industrial economics and information economics.

The second research program presented (in Chapter 3) is based on a less restrictive hypothesis about the firm's goal structure and assumes that other objectives beyond profit form part of the firm's utility function. It is also assumed that firms' preference orderings over interorganizational arrangements are different and that firms pursue objectives aimed at controlling resources and reducing dependence on external organizations. In other words, the firm seeks to maintain and increase its power in relationships with external actors (other firms and markets, government agencies, and so forth).

The central contribution to this perspective is Pfeffer and Salancik's (1978) *The External Control of Organizations: A Resource-Dependence Perspective* (henceforth abbreviated as RD). Pfeffer and Salancik's book makes use of concepts from various disciplines, but its dominant flavor is sociological. As comparison between the M&H and the RD perspectives considers conflict between these two approaches as a case of interdisciplinary conflict rather than a case of predictions' inconsistency on empirically testable grounds.

The third approach (presented in Chapter 4) analyzes processes that lead to the formation or genesis of organizational structures, in which organizational actors do not define any *a priori* preferences. Instead, organizational action is taken in a virtually random fashion, and preferences are learned *a posteriori*. Seen from this perspective organizational theory should thus explain organizational arrangements independently of any assumptions about *a priori* objectives.

This approach is useful in explaining solutions to organizational problems that emerge in cases where organizational actors do not have sufficient knowledge, attention, or time to solve them in any traditional means/ends sense. Such situations may occur in some decisionmaking areas of the firm or in institutions that deal with highly unstructured problems.

This perspective has been developed, using different methods, by James March and Karl Weick. It is grounded in the psychological and sociological components of organization theory and focuses on the study of organizations as knowledge and learning systems. Following the cognitive psychology approach, Weick and March stress the limits of a social actor's rational behavior. They study phenomena that can be viewed as attrition forces with respect to the means/end model of deductive rationality (such as perceptive biases, the unexpected consequences of action, circular cause-and-effect relations, and the irrational aggregate behavior of rational individual players). All traditional forms of rationality are criticized—the optimizing economic models of rational choice and also the satisficing models of bounded rationality. The interest here seems to lie in a more radical alternative form of rationality—drawing a contrast between *a priori* and *a posteriori* rationality and advocating a theory of action antecedent to thought for which preferences are learned by observing and evaluating the consequences of action. Applied to organizations, this form of retrospective rationality forms the basis for adaptive, trial-and-error processes whereby organizational structures are learned instead of being designed or calculated as a function of expected consequences.

As a research program Weick and March's approach has a less formalized structure than other approaches and does not seem to have been given an explicit title. I shall henceforth call their perspective the indeterministic perspective, which seems to reflect the authors' epistemological position.

The fourth perspective, presented in Chapter 5, goes beyond the question of what form of rationality on the part of the actors leads to the formation of an organizational structure. Here it is the rationality of the environmental mechanism of natural selection that leads to a process of structural adaptation.

According to the paradigm of biology, natural selection models are concerned with how better or superior forms of organization can be selected from populations of competing forms without assuming any hypothesis of conscious behavior on the part of the individuals in any given population. One perspective of organization studies, founded on the evolutionary theory as applied to human organization, is the population ecology of organizations (PEO) propounded by Hannan and Freeman (1977). These authors' dominant background is in mathematical sociology, and their approach was developed in institutions with traditions of positive scientific research, such as the University of California, Berkeley. The population ecology model has become popular in the managerial and organizational fields as the result of its business-oriented version put forward by Aldrich (1979).

Chapter 6 describes the organization and environment research program devised by Lawrence (1981) and Lawrence and Dyer (1983) as the new Harvard line of research on macrostructures. This program is basically a broad reformulation of the structural contingencies theory. It aims for synthesis among the different organizational perspectives that have proliferated in the last decade. However, as will be argued in Chapter 6, the new model developed by Paul Lawrence in collaboration with the historian Davis Dyer has some methodological shortcomings so that its heuristic power is not as strong as it might be. The industrial adaptation framework, as its authors call it, suggests that perhaps a premature synthesis was being sought or that the kind of synthesis being looked for was too vast to be achieved.

A framework for integrating the conceptual tools of organizational design is put forward in Chapter 7 and is based on the analysis of all these theoretical models. It addresses the metaproblem of how to choose a decisionmaking strategy for organization structure as a function of the organization's objectives and constraints. The point of view taken is that of a decisionmaker who is involved in solving organizational design problems. The models analyzed throughout the book are classified according to the goal structure that they attribute to the firm. The process of organizational choice, then, is viewed as a decisionmaking process that follows different paths according to the objectives of the decisionmaking system. The concept of contingent organizational decisionmaking processes has been developed more extensively elsewhere (Grandori 1984). Here it is applied to decisions that need to be made about organizational arrangements, and the decisionmaking process is seen as contingent on the state of knowledge about the expected consequences of organizational choices and the state of conflict among actors' interests.

NOTES

1. I refer in particular to European Group for Organizational Studies (EGOS) and to the review *Organizational Studies* edited by David Hickson.
2. In recent papers on the state of organization theory (Van de Ven and Joyce 1981; Rugiadini 1983) the field is characterized as having a multiplicity of different research programs whose relationships have not yet been clearly specified.
3. This second hypothesis is made much less explicit than the first by the proponents of this perspective. It is discussed here in Chapter 2.

1 CRISIS OF A PARADIGM

STRUCTURAL CONTINGENCY THEORY AS
A THEORY OF INFORMATION PROCESSING

Research on macro-organization structures in the 1970s was guided by the important contributions of Thompson (1967) and Lawrence and Lorsch (1967). These authors defined a set of propositions on environment/organization relationships that have come to be known as structural contingency theory (SCT). Considerable empirical research is based on the SCT framework; the main studies conducted on different aspects of the relationship between organizational structures and their environments include Perrow (1967, 1972), Mohr (1971), Duncan (1972), Galbraith (1970), Lorsch and Allen (1973), Kotter and Lawrence (1974), Lorsch and Morse (1974), Miles and Snow (1978), Mintzberg (1979), and Lane, Beddows, and Lawrence (1981). The central theorem of SCT can be expressed in two equivalent ways:

1. A firm's efficiency is dependent on the relation between the state of the environment and the form of the organization; or

2. Under conditions of efficiency, organizational form is correlated with the state of environment.

There is an important difference between this definition of SCT and the assertion that sometimes appears in the literature that organizational structure depends on environment. Structural contingency theory does not predict what forms will be observed—that is, the forms that firms will, or may, adopt in given environmental circumstances—but it does predict what forms will be efficient in those circumstances. Here is where the theory's normative value lies. For example, according to SCT, in a dynamic industry such as high technology many organizational forms may, and indeed will, exist, but the most flexible of them will be superior in efficiency. In fact, the nature of this organization/environment relationship, under conditions of efficiency, is a positive correlation between the degree of environmental uncertainty and the degree of flexibility in the firm's organizational form (that is, adaptation capacity and ad hoc problem-solving capacity).

This hypothesis, as has been said, has been well articulated and empirically developed in Lawrence and Lorsch's research (1967) and has a history dating back at least to March and Simon's seminal work *Organizations* (1958: 151), where they wrote that

> An individual can attend to only a limited number of things at a time. The basic reason why the actor's definition of the situation differs greatly from the objective situation is that the latter is far too complex to be handled in all its detail. Rational behavior involves substituting for the complex reality a model of reality that is sufficiently simple to be handled by problem-solving processes.
>
> In organizations where various aspects of the whole complex problem are being handled by different individuals and different groups of individuals, a fundamental technique for simplifying the problem is to factor it into a number of nearly independent parts, so that each organizational unit handles one of these parts and can omit the others from its definition of the situation.

This process, the differentiation of subgoals, is then reinforced by various cognitive mechanisms, such as individuals' tendency to selective perception—that is, to see in reality only things that conform to their own mental schemes; group pressure toward conformity in judgments; people's identification with their own professional group or organizational subunit; and selective exposure to information about the environment of those belonging to different parts of the organization: "salesmen live in an environment of customers; company treasures in an environment of bankers; each sees a quite distinct part of the world" (March and Simon 1958: 153). This is basic to the concept of *differentiation*, which is the first of two fundamental ingredients of organizational flexibility.

The second concept is *integration* (or coordination). If we design different specialized organizational units and assign different subobjectives to them (say, sales goals and production objectives for the same product), "we create in this way considerable interdependence and need for coordination among them." However, the authors (1958: 159–60) continue,

> Interdependence does not by itself cause difficulty if the pattern of interdependence is stable and fixed. For in this case, each subprogram can be designed to take account of all the other subprograms with which it interacts. Difficulties arise only if program execution rests on contingencies that cannot be predicted perfectly in advance. . . . The type of coordination used in the organization is a function of the extent to which the situation is standardized. To the extent that contingencies arise, not anticipated in the schedule, coordination requires communication to give notice of deviation from planned or predicted conditions, or to give instructions for changes in activity to adjust to these deviations. . . . We may label coordination based on preestablished schedules coordination by *plan*, and coordination that involves transmission of new information coordination by *feedback*. The more stable and predictable the situation, the greater the reliance on coordination by plan; the more variable and unpredictable the situation, the greater the reliance on coordination by feedback.

These planning and mutual adjustment (Thompson 1967) coordination devices will be needed to resolve the residual interdependence between subunits that remains once a number of strategies for reducing interdependence and unpredictability have been applied. March and Simon mention three main strategies for complexity reduction: the standardization of output (an uncertainty-avoidance strategy), the use of interchangeable operators (a reduction in the degree of labor division), and the maintenance of buffer inventories (March and Simon 1958: 160).

These points from March and Simon have been discussed at some length because they demonstrate how the main propositions of SCT derive directly from the cognitive theory of organizations as information-processing systems. All the main models of the contingency approach (Lawrence and Lorsch 1967; Thompson 1967; Galbraith 1973) develop different aspects of this same theory. These theoretical approaches will be considered here as a single set of coherent propositions about the analysis and redesign of organizations, which can be summarized as follows.

These perspectives all advance the proposition that if an efficient firm operates in a highly uncertain environment—that in general is operationally conceived as an industry—its organizational subunits will be highly differentiated in terms of structural profile as well as in terms of their managers' cognitive and emotional orientations.[1] More specifically, those subunits that are in contact with the most uncertain parts of the environment (such as marketing or R&D units) will have more flexible, decentralized, long-term–oriented and people–oriented internal organizational systems, as compared with subunits that have to cope with only internal problems or more stable segments of the environments. Such differentiated units in this flexible type of organization should be integrated by a complex mix of coordinational mechanisms, ranging from ordinary systems such as plans and programs to sophisticated means of coordination by feedback or mutual adjustment.

By contrast, efficient firms operating in more stable environments will exhibit less differentiated organizational units—with all units tending to be highly formalized, centralized, and specialized—and then will apply a simpler mix of integrating mechanisms, usually limited to programs and hierarchy.

The following sections selectively and summarily review the criticism directed at SCT since the late 1970s. They form the starting point for the development of more recent concepts about organizations discussed later in this book.

LIMITS OF THE PARADIGM AND THE BIRTH OF NEW THEORIES

Criticisms of the contingency approach share a common feature. They usually point out that other hypotheses may be as valuable as the SCT assertion that organizations adapt to the environment. Alternative processes and "moves" may also lead to successful survival of the firm. These ideas, not considered within the framework of SCT, can be classified into four categories.

1. A one-to-one correspondence between types of organizational structures and environment does not adequately represent the phe-

nomenon of organizational adaptation. A firm can adopt more than one *strategy* in most types of environment, whether certain or uncertain, and each strategy will lead to different consequences in terms of the efficient organizational structure required to implement it. It follows that firms should adapt their organizational forms to a strategically selected environment and not to a given inescapable objective environment. In addition, the rule that there is one best way of organizing for each type of environment (that a best-fit organizational form exists and should be adopted for each environment) is not easily justifiable, especially when the environment is characterized by *abundant resources*. In fact, if an environment is permissive (such as a protected industry, a low-competition niche, or a period of boom in demand), more efficient organizational forms can survive beside less efficient organizational forms in which there are abundant slack resources. The less fit structures can thus be maintained to the advantage of the firm's member (or of other external actors).

European researchers were among the first to stress that these variables had been overlooked within the structural contingency approach and to criticize it as an expression of the dominant deterministic and rationalistic orientation of U.S. culture (see Crozier and Friedberg 1977). For example, after having reviewed the work of Joan Woodward, Charles Perrow, Peter Blau, Derek Pugh, and David Hickson, Crozier and Friedberg (1977: 101 Italian ed.) conclude that the contingency approach has substantially transformed the one best way of classical theory (one optimal organizations model for all situations) into many optimal models as a function of organizational context. They assert that this

> empirical relativization of the one best way . . . in the best cases, is limited to the presentation of a series of statistical correlations between organizational structures (considered as dependent variables) and contextual factors. But these correlations say almost nothing about the only problem that matters, that is in what way, under what conditions and through what intermediating mechanism contextual factors affect and modify the rules of the game inside the organization. In the worst cases, this kind of research interprets correlations such as casual links and leads to an extremely mechanistic and deterministic conception of organizational change.

2. A prescriptive theory of adaptation should take into account what happens if a firm does *not* adapt. This is relevant because the cost of organizational change (such as the cost of overcoming struc-

tural inertia) may outweigh the expected benefits of adaptation or may simply be unaffordable. As already noted, if resources are sufficiently abundant or competition is weak enough, a firm can survive even though it earns less than optimal profits. By contrast, where firms operate in highly competitive markets in which large numbers of firms are dependent on the same scarce resources, and where these firms do not adopt organizational structures that fit this environment, they will be replaced by firms with better-fitting organizational forms. In other words, the adaptation process will occur by a *natural selection* of organizational forms where structural inertia blocks internal adaptive organizational change and where there is a sufficient external competition.

The role of biological analogies in organization theory seems not exhausted. Very interesting results have in fact been obtained from inquiring into the processes of natural selection in organizations. In fact, the role of this new biological analogy may be seen as a progressive one because it offers ways to avoid some errors made in the past in using biological analogies. There are at least two reasons for this. The first is that the variety of perspectives that exists today allows natural selection processes to be viewed as acting together with processes of deliberate choice of organizational forms, obviating the need to take a deterministic view. The second reason is that the population ecology is not the conventional biological model of organizations that asserts a possible or necessary best fit between an individual firm's organizational structure and its environment. Instead the model is a sophisticated version of the natural selection perspective, in which better-fit organizational forms outperform less fit forms within the context of many competing populations of organizations that are each characterized by a different form.

3. Firms can often change their environment instead of changing themselves, and this can occur in at least two ways: (1) They can select other markets—that is, they can diversify; or (2) they can try to modify the existing environment by trying to influence customers, suppliers, and competitors. The environment cannot be conceived as an inert and homogeneous object. It is, in effect, a set of other active organizations. Strategies of *influence on the environment* (or between organizations) are thus another alternative to internal adaptation.

A fruitful integration of existing organization theory and economic and sociological perspectives, developed outside the scheme of open systems, has played a major role in opening this window on interorganizational relations (Rugiadini 1983). In fact, the biological analogy of open systems (on which the theory of organization as systems that adapt to their environments is based) makes it difficult to see that organizations are capable of modifying their boundaries and influencing the shape and behavior of other systems because organic systems are not. New models that address the modification of organizational boundaries are then presented.

4. Adapting consciously to an environment (as well as exerting influence on it) requires that the environment and preferences be defined (that is, perceived and selected) in order to choose superior organizational solutions. But what happens if *a priori* information about the environment, or even about the firm's own preferences concerning organizational solutions, is poor? Some authors have argued that, where *a priori* information is scarce, fit organizational solutions cannot be designed or calculated *a priori*. They can be learned only through trial and error. In other words, where knowledge is lacking and can be acquired only by action, *organizational learning* processes are an alternative to rational choice between alternative organizational structures.

In the United States this organizational perspective (here called *indeterministic*) is being developed by James March and Karl Weick. Their views have led to an epistemological attack on the concept of the objective environment. This argument has been conducted from strongly subjectivistic positions, inspired by philosophers of knowledge such as Feyerabend (1975) and Berger and Luckmann (1966). The environment as an objective reality has been replaced by the concepts of ambiguity and of enacted environments. The following sections examine in more detail each of these limits of the traditional theory of organizational adaptation to environment.

THE ROLE OF STRATEGIC CHOICE AND THE CONCEPT OF UNCERTAINTY

If merely environmental characteristics are considered, there is no way to determine the most efficient organizational structure. Many paths may lead to a satisfactory performance by the firm (Simon 1969).

Different firms operating in the same industry may choose different strategies and organizational structures, and all may succeed. Indeed, as Child (1972) has forcefully argued, effective organizational forms are not uniquely determined or determinable by the environment, the technology of the firm, or its size. These factors may limit the set of feasible organizational solutions, but within that set organizational choices depend on the firm's strategic choices.

For example, suppose that two firms of approximately equal size and with the same basic production processes operate in the same mature industry. They might compete on costs and efficiency, which may be achieved through a highly formalized, specialized, and centralized organizational structure. However, they may choose a different strategy—for example, to innovate and compete in product differentiation and revitalization—which would require a flexible, decentralized, and integrated structure. On the one hand, this example demonstrates that strategic choice is important in determining structures (as the antideterministic critics of SCT have stressed), but on the other hand, it also shows that the question of strategic choice is not, strictly speaking, a limitation of a structural contingency view.

In fact, SCT is deeply rooted in the strategy/structure view of the firm, although it does not stress this aspect. If SCT is not interpreted too literally and mechanistically, the role assigned to strategic choice can be easily discerned. In fact, the environmental variables that SCT considers, are not as objective as might be assumed, and we are not obliged to draw from SCT's empirical results the same generalizations about organizational environment as its authors did. SCT's variables, which are intended to measure environmental uncertainty, not only describe a state of the external environment such as industry parameters but also record the effects of the firm's market strategies and technological choices. For example, SCT's degrees of uncertainty are measured through questionnaires asking people in different functions (marketing, production, R&D) to evaluate their tasks' perceived characteristics (such as information clarity, difficulty in performing their tasks, and time span of feedback) (Lawrence and Lorsch 1967). As Galbraith (1974) said more explicitly, the concept of environmental uncertainty in the SCT approach is actually represented by task predictability. The firm's strategic choices in, say, innovation policies, marketing positioning, and technical applications influence this variable as does the external environment (exemplified by customers, competitors, and products).

This methodology can be criticized because the operationalized variable (task predictability) is an inadequate measure of the concept of the external environment's uncertainty (Coda 1973; Pennings 1975). From an empirical standpoint, it also has been shown that degrees of uncertainty as measured in SCT are not closely correlated with objective indicators of environment volatility such as product and price variability (Tosi, Aldag, and Storey 1973).[2]

With hindsight, however, this ambiguity in defining SCT's subjective and objective measures of uncertainty may be considered more a strength than a weakness. The fact that SCT takes into account, whether deliberately or not, both environmental and strategic effects on structure may strengthen its main empirical results vis-à-vis some of the above-mentioned criticism about the role of strategy.

This ambiguity fosters a benevolent interpretation of SCT that counters the malevolent one put forward by Crozier and Friedberg and quoted above. In fact, instead of giving a theory its worst interpretation and searching for alternative models to that restricted formulation, it is possible to find a theory's best interpretation and then to extend and develop it further from that point.

This second approach—the best interpretation of the theory—is taken in this book. In this way, SCT can be interpreted as a model of how effective organizational structure is shaped by the strategy of the firm rather than only by its environment. When interpreted thus, firms that pursue a strategy of innovation—or of adaptation to market demand—select unpredictable tasks for themselves and should therefore have a flexible structure if they are to be successful. On the other hand, not *all* firms operating in a volatile industry should have a flexible structure because they may opt for a strategy other than adaptation to uncertainty.

In the same way, not all firms in a stable industry should have a mechanistic structure. Only if the firm bases its strategy on product specialization and growth in market share will it select by doing predictable tasks for itself, and it therefore needs a highly specialized and formalized structure if it is to perform successfully.

THE ROLE OF POWER OBJECTIVES
AND THE CONCEPT OF SLACK

In *A Behavioral Theory of the Firm* Cyert and March (1963) argue that many of the most interesting organizational phenomena occur because of organizational slack. Organizational slack can be defined as the amount of excess resources existing in an organization—that is, as "the difference between the resources of the organization and the combination of demands made on it" (Cohen, March, and Olsen 1972). Organizational slack also can be defined by referring to the classical theory of the firm. Under equilibrium conditions, organizational slack should be zero—that is, there should be no difference between the actual allocation of resources and the allocation of resources as a function of their marginal productivity (Cyert and March 1963; Williamson 1964).

The theory of organizations as information-processing systems postulates that the presence of free resources in the organization is critical to its survival in conditions of uncertainty (Galbraith 1974; March and Simon 1958). In fact, if the demands for resources utilization are not predictable and hence cannot be planned in advance, the demands can be satisfied where and when they arise by creating and using various forms of organizational slack. Inventory is an obvious and traditionally recognized form of slack resources because it absorbs uncertainty. Spare human resources (in terms of individuals' free time or unallocated time on the job) that enable energies to be devoted to problems as they arise according to need are a less visible and less recognized, yet important, form of organizational slack.

The traditional SCT model prescribes ways for firms to set up both physical and personal slack resources that allow highly flexible organizational structures to be formed that are able to cope with uncertain environments. These emerge most clearly from the version of SCT developed by Galbraith (1973, 1977). As he puts it, several organizational strategies may be used to enhance an organization's capacity to adapt to external demands that vary widely and frequently. Most of these strategies create some form of slack. They range from developing reserves of physical resources through inventory management, to leaving interaction between organizational units undefined, to a loose definition of the tasks assigned to individuals. These are all forms of slack (with respect to specific tasks' demands). As these tasks may vary continuously, however, it may not be possible to plan coordination between organizational units through programs. Coordination can be achieved only through mutual adjustment by exploiting the flexibility that slack physical and organizational resources provide.

Using slack resources in this way can effectively achieve a given organizational adaptation objective, although it is costly to maintain resources the specific utility of which cannot be determined in advance. Yet the maintenance of slack resources in a situation of uncertainty could be justified by an implicit comparison between their cost and the cost of determining and planning all the possible configurations of demand for the utilization of resources in an uncertain environment.

A second benefit that may be generated by organizational slack is *innovation.* Some slack provides the reserves needed to sustain trial-and-error innovation processes. If an entirely new set of problems arises, the expected benefits of a marginal resource unit invested in research and development cannot be calculated in advance. As March and Simon (1958) maintain and some researchers have subsequently confirmed empirically (see Lanzetta and Kanareff 1962; Payne 1976; Levinthal and March 1981), the cut-off point for these innovative research processes is given by the level of slack resources available more than by any calculation about the marginal productivity of research.

The role of slack resources has been considered within SCT only in relation to organizational adaptation and innovation capacity in the sense thus far discussed. However, slack also can be assessed in terms of other objectives. For example, financial, physical, and human resources do have a value for the individuals or the organizational units who control them, irrespective of the utility of such resources to the organization as a whole. The value that people put on resource availability is closely related to their own needs for power and freedom of action. It is thus very likely that individuals and groups in organizations will give a positive preference to slack resources. In other words it is reasonable to assume that organizational slack is one of the *objectives* of the member of the organization.

Although very important, the effect of organizational actors' power objectives on organizational structure has not been covered by SCT or in general in the information-processing approach to organizations. In fact, if one argues from the point of view of a firm seen as a single actor economizing on limited information-processing capacity, power can be assumed to be a dependent variable: The distribution of control over material and human resources and of discretionary decisionmaking among units should be a function of the location of critical uncertainties. Organizational units that deal with the most uncertain segments of environment *should* have more power because they control activities that are critical for the entire firm. A strict information processing approach will therefore prescribe a distribution of power that is efficient with respect to the economic objectives of the firm as a whole. The distribution of power is not conceived in a wider perspective as an efficient solution of a game[3] between players with different, independent, equally permissible preferences. Many scholars have consequently criticized the prescriptions of the SCT paradigm on the grounds that it has overlooked the power dimension, and a number of writers have begun to deal extensively with power in organizations (Pettigrew 1973; Bower 1970; Pfeffer and Salancik 1974a, 1974b; Hinings et al. 1974; Hickson et al. 1971). The theme of organizational power that had largely been absent in traditional organization theory (because it was left to sociology) has become one of the major topics in the organizational literature of the 1970s and 1980s.

Crozier's analysis of power as the foundation of organized action (Crozier 1963; Crozier and Friedberg 1977) has been central in this theoretical development. The main ideas put forward by Crozier and his colleagues have been developed starting with the distinction between actors' rationality and system rationality. The behavior of the system is then viewed as a game played by the firm's subsystems. Organization structure embodies the results of power negotiations as well as the rules of the game. The objectives of internal actors (individuals, groups, and formal units) are best represented by the goal of extending one's own power. The resources controlled and other power bases of each player are the first elements that have to be examined in order to understand the structure of the game that is being played. Of critical importance is the analysis of the replaceability of each actor's resources for other players, according to the tradition of dependence/relations analysis (Dahl 1957; Emerson 1962; Yuchtman and Seashore 1967; Jacobs 1974). This means that if controlled resources are to be a power base for one actor, they must be important (desired or necessary or critical) for other actors, and there must be few other sources from which the same resources can be obtained. Finally, in addition to structural power bases, a fundamental factor turns on how effectively power is exercised by actors through the choice of appropriate strategic moves and influence styles (Crozier 1963; Hickson et al. 1971; Pfeffer 1981).

Crozier's analysis of power has significantly contributed to the currently prevailing view of power in organization theory, in which power is seen as a relation between actors, not an attribute of any individual actor; and—synthetically defined—it resides in each player's control over a zone of uncertainty. In this view, organizational actors evaluate various possible organizational arrangements, taking into account consequences on their own power bases, and determine the structural solutions that are to be adopted through negotiation.

This perspective diverges from any hypothesis that contemplates that efficient structures will be determined by the environment. However, organization theory still seems far from any systematic theory about the effects of at least some principal types of organizational power game on organizational structure. It is not found in Crozier's writing or in subsequent contributions: Systematic thinking and investigation about how power games shape organizational structure remain a task for future research.

However, if we consider a more circumscribed perspective than that of the strategic analysis advocated by Crozier, there has been research on the effect of power objectives on organizational arrangements.[4] The studies concerned examine the effects of power objectives on the boundaries of organizational units and on interfirm boundaries and coordination mechanisms. In general, the result has been to show that organizational boundaries are larger when organizational members assign positive preferences to the resources allocated to them than when efficient boundaries are determined only as a function of economic efficiency (Pfeffer and Salancik 1978; see the section in this chapter on interdependence and interorganizational relations).

THE ENACTED ENVIRONMENT AND THE CONCEPT OF AMBIGUITY

The distinctive contribution of the indeterministic perspective on organization studies has been to extend the concept of uncertainty and to specify the implications for feasible organizational forms. The following analysis discusses how the wider concept of ambiguity, as defined by March and Weick in their recent work, relates to the traditional organizational concept of uncertainty.

The concept of uncertainty, as defined in the classic information-processing approach to the study of organizations, is comprised of three distinct variables. The first of these is task *variability*. In the traditional view, the environment is composed of known objects (clients, competitors, vendors, financial and research institutions, and so forth), but the mix of demands they make on an organization may vary in an unpredictable way. The second variable is *complexity*. If the number of environmental variables is very large, the limited information-processing capacity of any organization, however large or flexible, will break down at a certain point. The total amount of attention available in the organization simply will not be capable of considering all the relevant environmental variables and all their connections, with the result that environment will be perceived as uncertain. The third variable is *knowledge about cause-and-effect relationships* that link organizational actions and environmental conditions to relevant outcomes. It may well be that even if the configuration of environmental variables is known at a certain point in time, there are not sufficient theories, schemes, or rules-of-thumb to help predict the consequences of alternative organizational actions.

When analyzed in this way, uncertainty can be seen more clearly for what it is—namely, a state of *relations* between a knowing subject and an environment and not a state of the environment itself. It is the third variable, the knowledge of cause-and-effect relations, that best captures these roots of uncertainty as a problem of knowledge— that is, a problem of how to interpret an ambiguous reality. The two other variables derive instead from the more limited issue of information costs, which simply involves the relations between a given subject's limited information-processing capacity on the one hand and the amount of information that has to be dealt with on the other. The indeterminist approach has extended the concept of uncertainty largely in terms of the ambiguity of information and has focused on the problems of knowledge formation and change.

On the one hand, these authors have embarked on a detailed analysis of human cognitive processes with ambiguous information by drawing from psychology, sociology, and philosophy of knowledge. On the other hand, they have applied the notion of ambiguity (or uncertainty due to a lack of a single clear interpretation) both to cause-and-effect relationships and to other important elements of information processing in organizations, such as actors' preferences.

Regarding the concept of ambiguity, the indeterministic approach has stressed how perceptual distortion and subjective construction of reality have an influence on the process by which any actor defines an environment. In fact, the environment that an organization can respond to is, first of all, *perceived.* In other words, if it is conceded that a firm chooses to adapt to an environment, such adaptation is mediated in at least two ways: Subjectivity is reflected in selecting (1) an environment and a strategy to survive in that environment (choice of industries, market segments, product mix, and so on) and (2) stimuli, problems, and information that at any point in time are considered in that environment, whether consciously or unconsciously. For example, a firm can retaliate against competitors' moves, take opportunities to develop distinctive skills and expertise and exploit new technologies, or devote resources to new products, research and development, or other problems. It always will have to diagnose and select which problem to address among all those that happen outside (and inside) the boundaries of the organization. The environment of any organization thus can be only the environment of that particular organization because it is selected and therefore mediated by that organization's specific perceptual processes.

However, perception is only one aspect in Weick's (1979a) concept of enacted environment—an environment that is created and activated by organizations. This view contrasts with the dominant organizational concept of an inert environment. In Weick's (1979b) view the firm is a knowing subject with self-interest that constructs theories for social action by looking at social reality from the inside. The firm thus encounters all the typical difficulties in determining the object to be known—the outside reality or the environment—when that object is social and not natural, and these problems are compounded when the knowing subject, in this case, actually takes part in the process of both observing and modifying the environment. For example, consider price decisions in an oligopoly. Firms' forecasts about other firms' prices change the probabilities with which predicted events will in fact occur (these events are price decisions that take into account other firms' expectations). Or suppose that the choice of a price has positive consequences (it is rational choice) in a given configuration of the environment (where all other firms' prices are in a given position). The same choice may, however, be irrational if other firms also adopt the same price. Thus, the effect of both perception and interaction make it difficult to determine the cause-and-effect laws that regulate the organization/environment relationships, thus generating a state of ambiguity.

The second extension of the concept of uncertainty postulated in the indeterministic approach is the observation that unclear views by a subject about cause-and-effect relationships is not the only source of ambiguity. In organizational decisionmaking processes the technology may be unclear and so may the participants and their preferences (Cohen, March, and Olsen 1972). In other words, it may not be possible to define clearly the characteristics of the subject of social action itself. The relevant actors in organizational decisions may change over time and according to each particular issue, and their preferences are learned in this continuously shifting context.[5]

An important implication of this hypothesis of uncertainty about preferences is that organizational structure and processes cannot be designed as a means expected to produce certain effects that are positively evaluated by the decisionmakers. In these conditions, organizational solutions can be shaped only as a result of trial and error and social interaction—such as matches among actors, reciprocal learning of behavior and its consequences, and an *a posteriori* definition of preference based on observation of the outcome.

THE DIMENSION OF INTERDEPENDENCE
AND INTERORGANIZATIONAL RELATIONS

Suppose that a firm has a functional organizational form, that it produces and distributes a single product line (say, manufactured goods), that the end market for these goods is a mature industry, and that the firm has a substantial market share of these manufactured goods. This firm's environmental condition would be classified as stable in the framework of traditional contingency theory of organizations. It follows that, according to SCT, the firm would effectively coordinate its departments through communication, standardized procedures, and extensive planning.

Suppose now that the required characteristics of the goods that the firm produces become more specific and variable because new trends surface in the end-user market. According to SCT this state of increased uncertainty should trigger a conversion of the firm's internal organizational structure into a more flexible one. This would involve differentiating the organizational characteristics of departments to a greater extent and integrating them by mutual adjustment as well as by planning devices (Lawrence and Lorsch 1967; Thompson 1967).

However, this is not the only possible response. Within the SCT framework itself, Galbraith (1973, 1977) pointed out that the firm also can cope with more variable demand by maintaining a larger quantity of slack resources (in this particular example, by keeping larger product component inventories). This is the strategy that Thompson (1967) defined as buffering the technological core of the firm against environmental variability.

But an even more radical alternative to an uncertainty absorption strategy in which the structure is adapted (as opposed to an uncertainty avoidance strategy in which buffers are built) is to exert influence on the environment. As the new perspectives on interorganizational relations illustrate (Williamson 1975; Pfeffer and Salancik 1978), there are many other possible responses: interfirm mergers and demergers, joint ventures, associations, cartels, interlocking boards of directors, and informal coordination. Pfeffer and Salancik (1978) have asserted that if the idea of organizations as open systems is to be taken seriously, these strategies of environment negotiation and alteration must be analyzed and integrated into the theory, something that has not been done in the traditional open systems theory (which includes SCT).

An important consequence of considering interorganizational relations is that such organizational arrangements cannot be predicted and explained by environmental uncertainty alone. An information-processing dimension of environment alone cannot explain the choice *between* a strategy based on modifying the *internal* structure of a firm and a strategy that involves the changing *external* organizational arrangements; neither can it explain the choice between different interorganizational arrangements. At least one more dimension of the organization/environment relationship is needed: This is the type of interdependence that exists between firms. The premise that firms respond to environment uncertainty is contingent on firms' *dependence* on limited resources that exist in the environment (raw materials, capital, human resources, and customers) and on the fact that these may be and usually are controlled by *other* firms or institutions. Dependence on scarce resources is an important constraint on how many alternative organizational strategies are available to a firm that is undergoing a process of adaptation; adaptation also can occur as reciprocal adjustment among organizations rather than as a process of fitting to an environment.

Aldrich (1979) has explicitly advocated the need for combining the resource/dependence dimension and the information/uncertainty dimension in explaining organizational adaptation:

Consider, for example, the relationship between a manufacturing organization and its suppliers of an important raw material. The resource perspective may be brought together with the information perspective to formulate several testable hypotheses. When an organization interacts with others to obtain resources, it may face either an uncertain or certain relation, depending on the stability of the relations it has established with the interacting organizations, the assurances the latter provides of supplying the resources, and the effectiveness of its information gathering and interpreting apparatus. Even if assurances are given and a reasonable stable relationship exists, the interacting organization still has potential power over the focal organization—the manufacturing firm—because it cannot substitute for the resource nor obtain it elsewhere. Thus, dependence and uncertainty may vary independently of one another, and we can theorize about their joint impact on organizational autonomy and responsiveness. Note that certainty implies neither independence nor dependence—organizations can be certain about their dependence on others, as well as their freedom from dependence.

If it is assumed that uncertainty and resource dependence can be quantified in, say, two basic values—high or low—four basic configurations of organizations/environments relations arise (see Figure 1-1). In this enlarged framework, the traditional perspective (in which internal structures respond to external uncertainty) appears as a *special case* that is likely to occur only when there is considerable dependence on external forces. Only in these conditions will a firm in an uncertain environment have no choice other than to adopt a highly flexible organizational structure unless (and there is still another alternative) it can substitute or diversify the uncertain segments of its environment.

There are two major theoretical perspectives dealing with the problems of how to explain and design interfirm organization: the markets and hierarchies perspective (M&H) and the resource dependence perspective (RD) (discussed in Chapters 2 and 3). An attempt is made in this book to clarify the relationship between these two research programs, something that has not been done satisfactorily to date. Both perspectives deal to a large extent with the same subject matter—interorganizational relations. M&H uses concepts from information economics, while RD reasons in terms of resource dependence and power. However, it is argued here that the two perspectives use different languages but that their differences narrow when they discuss applied concepts (for example, central concepts in both models include interdependence *and* uncertainty). They also overlap considerably in some of their main predictions. For example, a basic prediction in both theories is that firms tend to merge if their trans-

Figure 1-1.   Combining the Resource Dependence and Information Uncertainty Perspectives on Environments: Conditions Affecting Organizational Responsiveness.

| | | Dependence on Other Organizations | |
		Low	High
Uncertainty in Relations with Other Organizations	Low	Maximum freedom from environmental constraints: lowest degree of responsiveness required (example: large manufacturer dealing with a small number of large suppliers)	Intermediate condition: must give into demands of others, but they are predictable (example: firm agreeing to a long-term contract with a monopoly supplier)
	High	Intermediate condition: freedom to switch to new organizations (example: manufacturer dealing with many small, struggling suppliers)	Minimal freedom from environmental constraints: greatest degree of responsiveness required (example: oil refineries during the 1973 OPEC crude oil embargo)

Source: Aldrich (1978).

actional interdependence is high and the context of their relationship uncertain.

The final section of Chapter 3 compares the two perspectives, recognizing the difficulty of translating into commensurable statements assertions drawn from theories belonging to different disciplines without distorting them too much. An additional difficulty in this particular case is that M&H uses the *normative* language of efficiency and prescribes superior organizational solutions in terms of their economic consequences but that RD follows the more *descriptive* approach of sociology. It seeks to explain the variety of existing organizational forms, not only those that are most efficient in terms of profit. For example, the resource dependence approach seeks to predict the circumstances that allow a firm to acquire other firms and integrate vertically with customers, thereby ensuring stable absorption of its output. By contrast, the M&H perspective is concerned with the circumstances under which this organizational solution will be efficient—that is, the extent to which the merged firm will outperform its two predecessors that were coordinated through the market mechanism.

It will be further argued that the differences between the M&H and RD perspectives on these questions of external organization are, in many respects, analogous to the differences between SCT and power perspectives on internal organization. Like SCT,[6] M&H in its current version does not consider control over resources as a possible objective. Both models prescribe structure as a function of economic efficiency. According to Crozier's school in Europe (and to RD), structures result from the strategies of organizational actors who strive to maintain and extend power by maintaining their independence with respect to other actors. The last parts of Chapter 2 and Chapter 3 propose some ideas on how to resolve these differences in internal and external organizational design.

THE NATURAL SELECTION ARGUMENT

There is another important objection to the thesis that organizational structures adapt to environmental contingencies. Existing successful organizational forms may not be chosen consciously by firms, and it is also possible that *firms* with less fit organizational forms *themselves become substituted* by firms with better-fit forms (Hannan and Freeman 1977). In other words, a process of adaptation between organizational structure and environments can occur at the level of competing *populations* of organizations, through the natural selection of those populations endowed with superior organization arrangements. The natural selection mechanism is likely to operate (as a substitute for internal adaptation) under conditions in which organizational change is being resisted by the many facets of the *structural inertia* phenomenon. Hannan and Freeman (1977: 931–32) provide a convincing list of these factors, which can be either internal or external to the firm. Internal factors include the specificity of investments and their inflexibility toward other uses, the unavailability of information about the emergence of new contingencies calling for adaptation, internal vested interest in the status quo, and the costs of innovation. External factors include entry barriers to different markets that limit adaptation through diversification, lack of information about these new markets, the vested interest of external actors in the continuance of the existing structure, and interaction effects that limit the chances of successful adaptation for all firms in an industry.

It should be noted, however, that a natural selection process need not be incompatible with conscious strategic choices made by firms about strategies and structure. The selection mechanism could work independently, whether the firms are acting consciously or not. As Aldrich (1979) has put it, the natural selection mechanism is indifferent about the sources of structural variations, whether they are the fruit of rational choice or of luck and chance.[7] The theory of population ecology of organizations postulated by Hannan and Freeman (1977) and developed by Aldrich (1979) is a natural selection model applied to business organizations and is presented in Chapter 5.

Some caveats should be mentioned that apply when interpreting this model if one is to avoid deterministic utilization of this new biological analogy. In the first place, a natural selection process neither implies nor guarantees that the forms selected are the optimal forms in the given configuration of the environment. It operates simply to the advantage of those forms that are superior to the others with respect to some attributes that are relevant in that environment. As Aldrich (1979) has emphasized, the natural evolution of organizational forms is toward better-fit solutions, not necessarily toward the best fit. In fact, the hypothesis that natural selection generates optimal solutions is legitimate only under very particular conditions—that is, only if the criterion of survival coincides with the criterion of economic efficiency, which, according to economic theory, represents conditions of perfect competition. By contrast, in conditions of less severe competition and incomplete information, there might be many relative advantageous positions that can be discovered by different firms. The selection mechanism will operate to favor first-mover firms that reach these positions first. The process of imitation and the spread of these successful solutions among other firms will provide an important retention mechanism (Winter 1971).[8]

A second caveat to be mentioned in making use of the natural selection hypothesis is that the process does not occur in a ubiquitous manner. As structural inertia can block adaptation, so can low competition block selection. Hannan and Freeman (1977: 940) point out that differential survival of organizational forms, in any given environment, will occur "as long as the resources which sustain organizations are finite and populations have unlimited capacity to expand."

NOTES

1. According to Lawrence and Lorsch's (1967) formulation, interunit organizational differentiation is measured using a number of attributes of organizational structure on the one hand and of managers' orientations on the other. Interunit structural differentiation is defined and measured by the difference in the degree of the various units' structuring of activities, verticalization of hierarchy and span of control, centralization of authority, and formalization of control systems. Interunit differentiation in managerial orientation is given by the dissimilarity in temporal orientations (short-term or long-term), in professional orientation (specialist or generalist), and in interpersonal orientations (production-centered or people-centered leadership styles) and by the difference in the subgoals that they are assigned (such as cost reduction in a production department, market share in a sales department, and product innovation in an R&D department).

2. Apart from this criticism, the findings of Tosi, Aldag, and Storey (1973) and of another study by Downey, Hellriegel, and Slocum (1975) show that there are also problems with the internal validity of the methods used for measuring the uncertainty variable. Downey et al. in particular explicitly come to reject the hypothesis that a firm's subjectively perceived uncertainty and the objective measures of industry uncertainty should necessarily be correlated. Instead they concentrate on the internal and external validity of the SCT questionnaire scales (as used by Lawrence and Lorsch 1967 and Duncan 1972) as measures of perceived uncertainty. These studies, although not conclusive because their results can be interpreted in various ways, suggest that there are at least some weaknesses in the empirical testing of SCT models.

3. The notion of an efficient solution of a game is used here in the same sense that it is used in game theory.

4. Crozier's concept of the strategic analysis of power has at least the same scope as the concept of strategic interaction advocated by Schelling (1960) and Goffman (1969), to whom Crozier refers.

5. These conditions of uncertainty are stronger than those allowed for in the traditional contingency theory, in which there might be task unpredictability but not preference ambiguity. Thompson (1967) already had had the intuition that there are at least two relevant dimensions of uncertainty in organizational decisionmaking processes: (1) uncertainty about cause-and-effect relations due to lack of knowledge and (2) uncertainty about preferences either due to lack of knowledge (experience) or lack of a clearly de-

fined collective preference in the organizational system (because of conflict among its parts). However, the implications of this hypothesis for organizational design were not worked out until they were developed by the indeterministic approach.

6. Although it does not consider reduction of resource dependence as a possible objective in organizational design, SCT considers interdepartmental interdependence as a determinant of an organizational structure designed to be efficient. Thompson (1967) postulated a well-known model for designing unit boundaries and interunit integrating mechanisms as a function of the type of interunit interdependence (see the second section of Chapter 2).

    The concept of dependence on external resources has virtually never been applied in traditional organization theory. The only important exception is the Aston Group research on a wide sample of institutions in the United Kingdom (Pugh et al. 1969a, 1969b). However, the Aston studies cover only the effects of dependence conditions on *internal* organization without looking at modifications to interorganizational relations (such as mergers or interfirm coordination agreements). Anyway, the discussion and criticism about how the concept of dependence was defined and operationalized in the Aston studies (Mindlin and Aldrich 1975; Donaldson, Child, and Aldrich 1975) have been useful in subsequent clarification of the concept and in the further development of studies on resource dependence.

7. Campbell (1960) has argued that a prerequisite for a natural selection model is that it be capable of explaining how successful adaptive innovations take place starting with purely blind variations.

8. Three mechanisms, or moments, are needed for a natural selection process to occur—variation, selection, and retention.

2 ORGANIZATION DESIGN WITH A SINGLE OBJECTIVE

This chapter focuses on approaches to organization design that seek to determine economically efficient organizational forms. The models presented here are drawn from the markets and hierarchies (M&H) perspective and from the hypothesis that the firm's preference function is represented only by profit. These basic theoretical assumptions belong to an information economics approach. Discussed here are the features of information economics as applied to organization design; the basic assumptions of the markets and hierarchies perspective; and how M&H is applied to the design of efficient boundaries and internal organizational arrangements of the firm. Finally, questions and points of debate are raised and discussed.

THE INFORMATION ECONOMICS APPROACH

Suppose that the firm can be conceived of as a decision system with a single objective—profit. The organizational structure of the firm then can be seen as a means to reach that end. This approach asks a basic question: In order to produce optimal economic actions, what should be the internal structure of the firm, taking into account that organizational structures and coordinating mechanisms have a cost? In fact, if the organization is seen as a means to an economic end, organization design may be seen as the problem of evaluating alter-

native coordination schemes in terms of their costs and of selecting the organizational form that produces economic actions with
the maximum expected net benefit (total benefit minus organization costs). Information economics and institutional economics
have addressed this problem which was neglected in conventional
economics.

For the moment, suppose not only that firms pursue a single
profit objective but also that they operate under conditions in which
they can behave as profit maximizers. In other words, suppose that
they have sufficient information to calculate their optimal economic
actions (such as prices and levels of output). Two models exemplify
this type of approach; one model determines the optimal internal
coordination systems, and the other determines the optimal size
(boundary) of the firm.

The first model is the *theory of teams* advanced by Marschak
(1954) and developed in Marschak and Radner (1972). A team is a
deciding system formed by multiple actors with homogeneous
preferences.[1]

Suppose that you are evaluating two alternative coordination systems for the team. One is a centralized scheme in which all relevant
information is sent to a central coordinator, who calculates the optimal actions that all the members should take and then communicates
these actions to the others. The other scheme is totally decentralized: Each member takes action independently (without communication) on the basis of the partial information that he has drawn
from the part of environment that he is in contact with. Assume
also that there is a common level of information-processing technology (for example, in the extent to which the information system is
computerized).

The problem of the choice of the superior coordination scheme is
solved by comparing the following types of information costs: (1)
the costs of transmitting all the information from and to the center
plus the cost of calculating the optimal actions for the centralized
scheme compared to (2) the costs of errors incurred in the decentralized scheme (that is, the magnitude of the differences between the
optimal action's benefits and the smaller benefit that might be generated by the various possible combinations of the members' independent moves). For example, suppose that a firm's income depends on
the combinations of prices and levels of output that the firm decides
to adopt. Suppose also that everybody knows the income conse-

quences associated with each combination of prices and quantities, and that the utility of the various levels of income is the same for both the sales department and the production department.[2] Then one can ask the following question: Is some integrating mechanism required, such as (1) a communication flow from departments to a center about all possible price/output combinations and their consequences, and a communication feedback about the calculated optimal actions to be taken or (2) a communication channel between departments so that they can converge on their best joint move? The answer depends on the organizational costs of each communication scheme that can lead to the desired outcome, compared with the expected value of the minor gains due to suboptimization when no integrating mechanism is adopted.

A variation of this problem is obtained when repeated decisions are considered. In this case, we can estimate the calculation and communication costs of reaching the optimal action in only one move and compare this cost (or decision time) with the cost (or time) that would be necessary to reach the optimal action through sequential corrections of the partial independent moves operated by the departments by themselves, on the basis of the observed results of their choices (see also T. Marschak 1965, 1972; Radner 1972).

The second model, developed here more fully as an example of the economics of organization approach, is the model for determining the size of the firm by taking into account organization costs that were elaborated by Williamson (1970). To consider organization costs, Williamson defined the difference between revenue and costs (that is, profits) that the firm is to maximize as a function that includes both the conventional variables of output, production costs, and prices but also the costs of hierarchy and coordination mechanisms necessary to produce those outputs and decisions.

The following variables were considered by Williamson to represent organization costs. First, the span of control,[3] defined s, is considered, and it is supposed to be constant for any supervisory position in the organization. Then, the number of hierarchical levels, called n, is considered an indicator of the organizational size of the firm. When the organization size increases in order to produce higher levels of output, hierarchical and coordination expenses also increase for at least two reasons. First, there are increasing losses in efficiency due to control loss phenomena: The organization members do not comply perfectly to communications and orders, either because of perceptual problems or because of goal conflict. These control loss phenomena are represented in the model by a parameter α that expresses the rate of compliance of people who received instructions. Second, when n increases, organizational costs increase because of the need to differentiate salary levels at different hierarchical levels: The ratio of the two salaries w_i/w_{i-1} at any two consecutive hierarchical levels i and $i-1$ is expressed in the model by the parameter β. Given these parameters, the problem of the optimal size of the organization can be solved. The optimal size is the value of n that maximizes a profit expression in which both costs and the level of output are functions of n, s, and α.[4]

The model also can be used to study the *variations* of the optimal organization size n^* as the other parameters vary. With this model, Williamson has shown that the optimal organization size increases as

1. The rate of compliance increases;
2. The span of control increases;
3. The ratio of the basic wage (w_0) on the margin on nonwage costs decreases.

These results suggest that, other things being equal, organizational optimal size is larger, first, when there are fewer communication distortions and decays. This might occur, for example, when there is a strongly shared organizational culture and a low goal conflict at different hierarchical levels. Second, efficient organizational size is larger when it is possible that many individuals depend on the same supervisor (as when tasks are routinized) or when the total labor costs in the least qualified position is lower (a case that might be represented by a capital-intensive rather than a labor-intensive type of production).

Such models of organization design have at least one important feature in common with conventional economics—that is, the assumption that firms do optimize. Thus, the domain of these models is limited to predictable market and production conditions and to simple quantitative organizational variables so that their costs and benefits can be evaluated and compared.

The more recent contributions to the economics of organization by Williamson (1975, 1981) define a wider approach that does not involve, strictly speaking, optimization of organizational variables. This approach compares the *costs* of alternative organizational forms that are both capable in principle to regulate and control the same activity. This approach, the transaction costs approach, is the basic frame of the organizational research program called markets and hierarchies (M&H), which is presented in the remaining part of this chapter.

THE MARKETS AND HIERARCHIES APPROACH

Basic Assumptions

The main ideas about uncertainty and its role in the markets and hierarchies approach (or organizational failure framework) are drawn from Simon's thought. Uncertainty is important because of the limited human capacity for information processing (Simon 1945, 1957). In the presence of uncertainty, the hypothesis of a perfectly informed and perfectly rational decisionmaker—which is the fundamental requirement of the ideal performance of markets—fails to hold. In fact, a state of uncertainty is a type of relationship between an actor and a decision context in which, by definition, it is logically impossible or too costly for the actor to perform a number of logical operations, such as foreseeing all future circumstances that might influence decisions' outcomes, assigning probabilities to those outcomes, considering all possible courses of action to reach them, comparing all these alternatives as measured on some common utility scale. When economic transactions occur in turbulent environments that are disturbed by frequent exogenous unpredictable shocks, or within competitive structures that do not lead to easily predictable equilibria, it is difficult to make all the above-mentioned computations and judgments.

By contrast, the market, as a form of regulation of economic transactions, requires full transparency in the information flows. More precisely, it requires that prices convey all the information needed in order to make an exchange decision. According to the elegant formulation of Hayek (1945) quoted by Williamson (1975: 5), "the marvel of the economic system is that prices serve as sufficient statistics, thereby economizing on bounded rationality." In other words, if we admit as given that human capacity for information processing is finite, a market system can govern exchanges if economic quantitative indicators represent all attributes of goods or services that are relevant for the involved parties.

Market-failure events occur whenever prices become unreliable and ambiguous information. Moreover, there are other conditions that drive markets from the perfect-competition model. These circumstances have been carefully argued in the economic literature on market failures.[5]

Besides being caused by uncertainty about the consequences of actions due to unpredictable contingencies and unreliability or unavailability of price information, market failure might also occur because of

The presence of technical indivisibilities or economies of scale (such as increasing returns to production scale or discontinuities in the quantities of output that can be produced);

The presence of externalities (for example, consequences of a transaction are borne by third parties not involved in the exchange, or exchange decisions depend on considerations that are external to the transaction in question—for example, they are based on comparisons among producers or consumers);

The presence of asymmetries in knowledge or substitutability so that one party can unilaterally influence prices and other exchange conditions.

The markets and hierarchies perspective argues that, where market failure conditions prevail, the hierarchical form of governing transactions within the boundaries of a single firm is a feasible, more efficient alternative.

Hierarchies are powerful means for reducing uncertainty: A hierarchy's rules, job descriptions, and incentive and control system make the internal world much more predictable than the external one (Simon 1945); and a hierarchy reduces complex problems to manageable parts (March and Simon 1958). Uncertainty and bounded rationality lie at the heart of the existence of organizations (March and Simon 1958).

Uncertainty, however, as well as other factors that lead to a "wrong" functioning of markets, are not sufficient to provoke substitution of a system of external exchanges for an internal system of central regulation. The resulting determinant of the choice of internalizing, within a single firm, transactions previously completed in the marketplace, is the coupling of uncertainty about the terms of exchange and a relative nonsubstitutability of the partners of exchange.

A variety of factors can promote shifting from a previously existing "perfect" substitutability of partners or can create a relationship of quasi-indispensability, reciprocal dependence, or, to use Williamson's word, *idiosyncratic* exchange. These factors include the learning-by-doing phenomenon, for which already experienced parties are preferred to any other party because they are known; the requirement of specific knowledge to perform a transaction, which implies long periods of training and collaboration with the partner; natural monopoly situations; and first-mover advantages. These factors can raise substantially the cost of a substitution of one or both parties in a transaction.

Williamson (1975) calls this case of low substitutability the small-numbers condition. It is contrasted to the large-numbers case that characterizes perfect market conditions. Small numbers and uncertainty together are the basis of that explosive mixture that is determinant for the collapse of the market and the emergence of a hierarchical form of governing transactions. On the one hand, uncertainty precludes the possibility of stipulating comprehensive contracts that specify all possible contingencies;[6] and on the other hand, low substitutability makes it difficult for any one party to sanction effectively the other for not respecting the spirit of contract and for exploiting unfairly its unavoidable ambiguity. Therefore, Williamson argues, under these conditions normal self-interest–seeking economic behavior is likely to degenerate in a propensity to self-interest–seeking with guile, which he calls *opportunism.*[7]

An actor is said to pursue his interest with guile if he is prone to make use of "false or empty—that is, self-disbelieved—threats and promises" (Goffman 1969). Opportunism—in the sense of a propensity to exploit all the opportunities to get more out of an exchange, even when the actions taken are not fair or ethical—is considered by Williamson a basic characteristic of human economic behavior. Integrating the concept of opportunism with bounded rationality leads to a fuller understanding of economic behavior and organization structures. This is not to imply that opportunism occurs in every case of economic behavior as an endemic disease. It occurs when it is difficult to devise and implement the control and enforcement mechanisms that relieve pressure on the limited resource of honesty, in the same way that when it is difficult to predict outcomes and analyze alternatives, pressure is created on the limited resource of rationality.

The Efficient Boundaries

Uncertainty and small numbers are properties of the relationship between an organization and its environment. According to the M&H perspective, these relationships are conceived of as the set of economic transactions that a firm has with other firms in the environment. The transaction is an elementary unit of analysis in industrial and institutional economics (Coase 1937; Commons 1934): "A transaction occurs whenever a good or service is transferred through a technologically separable interface" (Williamson 1981: 552).

It is generally important in organization design to specify an elementary unit of analysis because it enables the actor to choose among different ways of aggregating elementary tasks into more complex ones. In the M&H perspective the elementary units are transactions, and the main aggregation problem is whether to assign activities to different economic units and regulate the transfer on the market or to regulate 'the whole transaction inside the firm. A second aggregation problem, or more properly, another boundary design problem that is addressed in the perspective—is the design of the boundaries between *internal* units. The M&H perspective resolves these two aggregation problems in an analogous way.

Insofar as internal boundaries between units are concerned, M&H reaches the same conclusions and uses approximately the same reasoning as the traditional structural contingency theory, particularly the formulation of Thompson (1967). Thompson analyzes input/output relationships or types of transfer between elementary separate units. He calls this *interdependence*, and this variable provides the criterion for aggregating activities so that the costs of coordination are minimized. When the output of an activity is an input for another, we have a simple transaction or serial interdependence that can be regulated by ordinary programs and procedures. Where the reverse is also true—and the output of each activity is the input for the other—we have reciprocal interdependence, and the regulation of that transaction requires more complex coordination mechanisms. In fact, in order to perform any of the mutually interdependent activities well, rich and abundant information is needed about each activity (as, for example, in developing a new sophisticated product). When analyzing organizational units' design, Thompson observed that the cost of an organization is higher when it separates highly interdependent activities and then sets up complicated mechanisms of continuous adjustment between these activities than the cost is when the organization aggregates activities linked by the most uncertain and intense interdependences inside the same unit and then resolves residual interdependences by simpler mechanisms of lateral relationship.

Designing interunit boundaries as a function of transaction costs produces the same results. Williamson (1981), in fact, develops the same argument with respect to the "design of the efficient boundary of an operating unit," making explicit the analogy with Thompson's ideas. As Williamson stated (1970), organization costs are raised unnecessarily whenever decoupling possibilities between loosely interdependent activities are not exploited and, conversely, whenever highly interdependent activities are separated, so that the probability that the system will produce correct outputs is decreased or costly integrating mechanisms have to be set up.

However, Williamson argues, activities cannot be aggregated only on the basis of transaction (or coordination) costs. A trade-off is needed between them and production costs: In fact, aggregating interdependent activities saves coordination costs, though it might generate losses in terms of economies of scale and specialization. Consequently, efficient organizational boundaries depend on the level of total costs—transaction costs plus production costs. These total costs must be estimated for different organization schemes, and the lowest-cost scheme chosen.

One may observe—as Williamson (1981) polemically does—that the trade-off between coordination costs and production costs were not stressed by Thompson. It also should be recognized, however, that it has been well outlined and articulated in other contributions of SCT (see, for example, Galbraith 1971). It is then safe to conclude that the organization design concepts of the transaction cost approach and of the structural contingency approach, as applied to the *internal* organization problem that both models address, are equivalent and interchangeable.[8]

34   PERSPECTIVES ON ORGANIZATION THEORY

The problem of make or buy, or the problem of the efficient boundary of the firm, is analogous to the problem of establishing internal boundaries. Williamson (1981) presents a clear formal exposition of his main argument: The threshold of organizational failure, or the indifference point between a market and a hierarchy, is given by the equation $\Delta PC + \Delta TC = 0$, where ΔPC is the difference between production costs in the two alternative arrangements of internal production (hierarchy) and external production (market), and ΔTC is the difference in transaction costs under the market and under the hierarchical forms of regulation.

The organizational failures framework hypothesizes that the two variables ΔPC and ΔTC vary as functions of three independent variables that characterize the transaction in question: (1) the specificity of the investment required to execute the transaction; (2) the level of uncertainty that characterizes the context of the exchange; and (3) the frequency at which the transaction is repeated. Of course, as Williamson (1981) points out, other independent variables may well affect the efficient boundaries. For example, he cautions that ΔPC surely depends on the volume of production. Consequently, in studying the variations in the relative magnitude of production and transaction costs due to any single independent variable, other things should be assumed to be equal.

Williamson, then, concentrates his attention on the study of ΔPC and ΔTC as functions of investment specificity (called A). Implicitly other variables—namely, the uncertainty and frequency of transaction—are held constant. Investment specificity is a variable that is both an antecedent and an operationalization of a small-numbers condition (the more the specificity, the less the number of possible substitutes of any of the parties in the transaction). Assume that the functions $\Delta PC = f(A)$ and $\Delta TC = f(A)$ have the shape represented in Figure 2-1 (Williamson 1981). Then point A^*, where the sum function $\Delta PC + \Delta TC$ is zero, represents the threshold of resource specificity beyond which, other things being equal, hierarchy (the internal organization of that transaction) becomes superior to market (the external exchange of the goods or services among mutually substitutable firms).

Williamson's argument opens by assuming that "at the beginning there were markets." Markets can be sustained as long as economic actors remain substitutable—that is, resource specificity remains near

Figure 2-1. Determination of the Indifference Point between Market and Hierarchy as a Function of the Specificity of the Investments Required in Transactions.

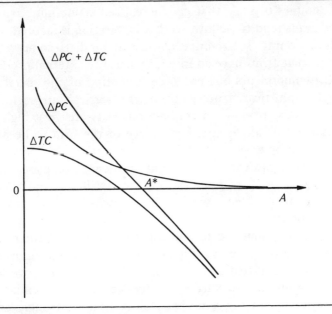

Source: Williamson (1981).

to zero. This is true even if there is uncertainty and transactions are recurrent.

However, resource specificity may be greater than zero for certain transactions or may become greater than zero even where it was not in the past. Examples of the first case are highly specialized productions, with applications that are strictly specific to certain other goods (such as specialized components of sophisticated aircrafts or high-quality weaving used only by particular fashion houses), so that the two parts in the exchange are nearly nonsubstitutable. An example of the second case occurs when conditions of nonsubstitutability are created by reciprocal learning by doing of the two partners, so that once an exchange relationship is started it easily becomes privileged with respect to any other. In both these situations, in Williamson's words, parties are locked into the transaction, develop idiosyncratic competences toward each other, and evolve toward a bilateral monopoly. Under these conditions, the expected costs of opportunistic behaviors of the counterpart are very high, and the market relation becomes inefficient with respect to hierarchical control. Moreover, Williamson adds, where resources are highly specialized, the economies of scale that can be realized maintaining separate specialized firms tend to be low, so that integration is favored.

This reasoning is attractive because it predicts some well-known solutions that firms have adopted, such as the external production of standard components but not the production of the specific, differentiated, sophisticated products; or the vertical integration of sales forces into the firm when transaction costs are very high (specific competences of sale agents, high image of the firm to be protected, relevant consequences of sellers' opportunistic behaviors). However, Williamson's argument raises several problems. Some are definitional problems and issues of emphasis on the variables in the model; some are conceptual problems, which will be discussed in the next sections of this chapter.

For example, here we followed the exposition of the transaction-cost approach discussed in Williamson's 1981 article because it clarifies two important features of the model that are often overlooked in other literature in the M&H perspective. In fact, Williamson and other authors with the same perspective usually strongly emphasize how the small-numbers condition affects the firm's efficient boundaries rather than other transaction characteristics. By contrast, the effects of these other variables, especially uncertainty and transaction frequency, may be very important. For example, we would not find any stimulus toward internalizing (buying) the only supplier of a complex highly specific equipment if our need (hence, the transaction) is not recurrent. Neither would we produce internally if the final market is stable or controlled enough and the supplier's eventual underperformance on time and quality is not critical. A correct application of the transaction costs approach then should lead to design the efficient boundary as a function of all the relevant sources of transaction costs, not only investment specificity. As Williamson (1981) mentions briefly, uncertainty and frequency effects on the efficient boundary could be studied (other things being equal) in the way that the case of specificity was studied. Holding investment specificity constant, the firm's boundaries should be larger where uncertainties affecting the transaction are more intense and numerous and where transaction frequency is higher.

A second point is that M&H authors' arguments[9] can be mislead-ing because of their emphasis on transaction costs with respect to production costs (Williamson's 1981 article again is an exception here). No matter how high the transaction costs that uncertainty and specificity generate, in many cases the costs of internal production can be much greater.

A third criticism frequently raised about the M&H approach is that transaction costs are not operationally defined. In other words, the research program has not yet specified how to measure its cen-tral concept and determine the relevant categories of transaction costs. This objection is important, but it is a technical, rather than a conceptual consideration. In other words, the fact that a concept has not been made operational in the early stage of development of theoretical perspective is not a reason to reject the theory.

Some work is already available in the direction of a better opera-tionalization of the OFF. Anderson and Weitz (1983), for example, have worked out a questionnaire for the measurement of transaction and production costs relevant for vertical integration in the market-ing function. Examples of typical costs of transactions regulated through markets (which could be measured empirically) include

1. Lack of contractual formulas and enforcement tools that can guarantee conformity to time and quality standards;
2. Difficulties in measuring and controlling the actual performances of other firms;
3. Difficulties in finding substitute competence in the market be-cause of long and idiosyncratic training cycles;
4. Needs for reservation about know-how information.

Typical and measurable costs of transactions that are regulated through hierarchy include

1. Difficulties in defining reward systems that favor the desired behaviors;
2. Difficulties in measuring and controlling the actual performances of peripheral units;
3. Structural costs (number of positions, salary structure differen-tiation, information and control systems complexity).

The analysis of this second group of transaction costs has been neglected thus far by the M&H approach. Most work has concentrated on the costs of markets rather than of hierarchies. This choice, explicable in terms of the dominant economic background of the authors, has considerable practical importance for the organizational solutions that are actually reached by these authors. Hierarchy, in fact, often is prescribed wherever market transaction costs are high, almost as if a hierarchy were an ideal bureaucracy with zero internal transaction costs.

In principle however, the variable of hierarchical costs is included in the transaction-cost model. The point is to examine in a deeper way the hypothesis that hierarchies, as markets, are not frictionless systems and to develop internal transaction cost and hierarchical failures analysis. The next section elaborates on this issue.

The Costs of Hierarchy and the M-Form Hypothesis

The threshold beyond which a hierarchical form becomes superior to a market form depends not only on the level of transaction and production costs under the market system but also on internal transaction and production costs, under the assumption that the same transactions are regulated through a hierarchical form. Therefore, in order to determine which form is actually superior (internal or external), we should measure not only external transaction costs but also the maintenance costs (and eventually the set-up costs) of an internal organizational structure—including the costs of those opportunistic behaviors that are typically generated by hierarchical structures. In the main M&H contributions, the issue of analyzing and measuring internal costs is underexamined, even though the trade-off is clearly outlined in formal terms within the equation for calculating the threshold of market failure.

Williamson's main argument is that when conditions of exchange depart from those of perfect market, transaction costs (and eventually also production costs) under the market form of governance increase. At the same time the convenience of setting up and maintaining an internal structure increases because the firms' interdependencies increase. The hierarchical form is supposed to achieve superior efficiency with respect to the market relationship because (1) there is reduced conflict of interest between parties because consistent goals will be assigned by a central authority; (2) the possibility exists of resolving emerging conflicts by fiat rather than through costly and time-consuming negotiations; (3) there is better access to information about the parties' actual operating conditions and performance; and (4) there is increased uniformity in perceptions and expectations that reduce the likelihood of judgmental and cultural conflicts (Williamson 1975, 1979).

A problem with these assumptions about the comparative advantages of hierarchy is that a hierarchy has these properties only when it is a pure, bureaucratic, centralized, frictionless machine, in the style of the Weberian ideal type. However, hierarchies depart from their pure types in the same way that markets depart from the perfect-competition model. And internal transaction costs may impair the distinctive hypothetical advantages of hierarchies over markets. For instance, within organizations we typically find suboptimizing behaviors, low transparency and strategic misrepresentation of information, nonfeasibility of conflict resolution styles based on imposition or fiat, differentiation of cognitive styles and perceptual conflicts. Organizational literature and experience supporting these facts abounds. And in M&H there is a clear acknowledgment that these organizational costs increase to the extent that at least two major independent variables increase: the size of the firm and the rate of conflict among internal particular objectives.[10]

Therefore, the main M&H argument is not to be interpreted as asserting that if there are high transaction costs on the market because of transaction high specificity and uncertainty, then hierarchy should be preferred. The relative superiority of the two forms of management, even in specified conditions of small numbers and uncertainty, cannot be decided once and for all. Empirical estimates of the comparative costs are required, and the solution will depend on the costs of the specific type of hierarchy that is designed and implemented in the particular case. Among these costs, we should consider not only those generated by the size that the firm has achieved but also the expected increase in internal transaction costs caused by the internalization of new activities. These marginal internalization costs may be very high (especially when large-firm mergers are involved), and they are likely to vary with both the size of the existing hierarchy to be expanded and with it shape.

This last hypothesis is related to the so-called multidivisional hypothesis advanced by Williamson (1970). Although in later M&H contributions on the multidivisional issue (Armour and Teece 1978; Burton and Obel 1980) the problem of choosing between alternative internal organizational schemes has been addressed as a problem separate from the efficient boundaries problem, the two problems are seen here as related, as in Williamson's early theorizing.

Now we turn to the evaluation of the effect on efficient organizational boundaries of the two main internal organizational schemes: the functional structure or U-form (unitary form) and the divisional structure or M-form (multidivisional form).

Assume, as the initial condition for a hypothetical development pattern, that a firm starts with a simple hierarchy or elementary structure.[11] A single-position, centralized decision unit coordinates through one-way, top-down communications a number of operational units with narrow discretionary domain. As firm size increases, two categories of internal transaction costs increase: One is generated by limitations in information-processing capacity; the other is generated by structural conflict of interest. In the first case, the number of communications within the system will increase with size, and, with it, the amount of control loss due to perception biases and to reinvention, misrepresentation, and decay of the transmitted messages. As to conflict of interest, the number of organizational units and interunit differentiation will increase with size, and this will increase the control loss due to deliberate noncompliance and individual subgoal pursuit. The growth of a simple hierarchy reaches a limit—its efficient boundary—when the marginal costs of control losses outweigh the marginal benefits of a further expansion of the scale of operations.

This limit on organization size can be shifted upward by changing the shape of internal structure through decentralization of authority and delegation of functional responsibilities. Changing from an elementary to a functional structure, a firm will be able to sustain further expansion efficiently. Functional departments will act autonomously and communicate directly with each other on operation matters; many of the communications with the center are saved, replaced by planning mechanisms and systems of partial objectives and incentives.

Different types of transaction costs, however, typically arise in functional structures—costs that in turn determine new limits on organization size. These costs are generated mainly by the professional and power subgoals pursued by the functional departments' managers (that is, sales, production, R&D, and so forth).[12] The maximum size that a firm can efficiently reach can be further shifted by resorting to a particularly decentralized form of hierarchy; this is the M-form enterprise, an intermediate form between a hierarchy and a market. In fact, it is possible to exploit the decoupling properties of a hierarchy when the interdependencies among its parts are sufficiently weak—for example, when there are different product lines, market segments, or geographical areas that do not share related activities. In this case the activities can be efficiently organized as independent quasi-firms, provided that the savings in communication and coordination costs are higher than the costs of the unmanaged interdivisional interdependences and of the underexploited functional economies of scale and specialization (Galbraith 1971; Williamson 1970).

Moreover, as the M-form hypothesis asserts, a multidivisional form should allow transaction costs economies due to lower internal opportunism because it is possible to devise reward schemes based on the different divisions' profitability. This would reduce the divisional managers' incentives to elusive, discretionary, or otherwise opportunistic behavior. Other things being equal, efficient firm size under a multidivisional governance form should therefore be larger than under a functional form.

The entire argument is shown in Figure 2-2, which summarizes how some main categories of hierarchical costs affect the efficient boundaries of the firm. For example, consider the acquisition problem of large firms. Acquisition may be inefficient if the buyer is already a large company and is functionally organized. It may be efficient, even beyond that size, if the buyer firm has a multidivisional organizational structure because the acquired firm may be added as a separate unit instead of being integrated into other pre-existing functions.

The economizing properties of transaction costs attributed to the M-form have led to the M-form hypothesis in the following more general and stronger terms: "the organization and operation of the *large* enterprise along the lines of the M-form favors goal pursuit and least-cost behavior more nearly associated with the neo-classical profit maximization hypothesis than does the U-form organizational alternative" (Williamson 1970: 134, italics added).

This proposition is perhaps the only part of OFF that has gained reasonably wide empirical support. In fact, this hypothesis offers a rational or causal explanation for the historical evolution of large U.S. enterprises, as described by Chandler (1962). Williamson's theo-

Figure 2-2.   Effects of the Costs of Hierarchy in Different Organizational Forms on the Firm's Efficient Boundary.

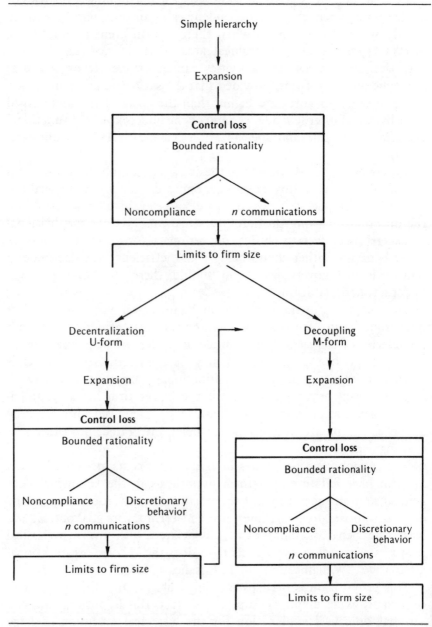

retical assertions find an empirical base in Chandler's research to "predict in retrospect" (to use the language of the philosophers of science). Further, the M-form hypothesis has been tested with some success both in field research (Cable and Steer 1978; Teece 1981b; Armour and Teece 1978) and through computer simulation (Burton and Obel 1980).

It should be noted, however, that this version of the M-form hypothesis has raised some debate because of its apparent universalism (Pfeffer 1982; Teece 1981b). It is in fact possible to interpret the hypothesis as asserting that the M-form is generally or always superior to the U-form.

This universalistic interpretation, though, is not in fact supported by available evidence and theory; it can be attributed to the format in which the hypothesis has been presented. First, Williamson's hypothesis of the superior efficiency of the M-form refers to the *large* U.S. enterprise—that is, a typically diversified firm in which the main contingency criteria (such as system decoupling properties and positive trade-offs with diseconomies of scale and specialization) are likely to be satisfied. Second, from an empirical standpoint, the same observation seems to hold true: Most empirical studies on this issue have tested the long-run superior profitability of M-form over U-form enterprises in the case of large, mostly diversified, firms.

Third, a universalistic interpretation of the M-form hypothesis would be contrary to the spirit of the organizational failures framework. A fundamental message of the transaction-cost approach is that it is not possible to determine once and for all which organizational form is superior in efficiency—whether one considers the extreme or pure alternative forms (perfect market versus the U-form, centralized, full bureaucracy) or analyzes the comparative efficiency of intermediate forms (divisional structures, holdings, franchising arrangements, federations and associations, and so forth).

Finally, a general assumption of the transaction-cost approach is that all hierarchical forms, M-form included, have a finite capacity for information processing and therefore that beyond a certain size level internal organizational failures are to be expected because of control loss phenomena. With specific reference to large divisional structures, it has been argued (Boulding 1968; quoted in Williamson 1970) that top managers live in imaginary worlds that are painted by the men and women who live in contact with the environment. Even not considering corrupted forms of divisional structure (Williamson 1975),[13] an intrinsic motive for expecting discretionary behaviors in pure M-form organizations is that divisions control a good part of the information on which rewards and resource allocations are based. Bower's (1970) research on the role of divisional power subgoals in the resource allocation processes of large divisionalized companies is a good counterexample to the hypothesis that M-form organizations behave without friction, in a profit-maximizing way, at any size level.

Hierarchical Failures and the Clan Form

As discussed in the preceding paragraph, the invention and adoption of decentralized organizational structures can extend the conditions of survival of hierarchical forms. The decentralization of internal structure diminishes the control loss failures due to the growth of a hierarchy, other things being equal. Among these other things, however, are factors that might have a powerful effect on efficient boundaries. Perhaps the most important of these variables is the degree of congruence among objectives and interests of different internal individuals and groups—that is, the rate of compliance within the organization. The higher the level of congruence among organizational objectives (the higher the rate of compliance)—ceteris paribus— the lower internal transaction costs will be (Williamson 1970) (see the first section of this chapter).

The distinctive contribution of William Ouchi (1979, 1980) to M&H is the study of the clan form of governance of transactions—an organizational form based on high conformity among members' basic objectives and interests.

A clan can be seen as an alternative mode of organizing, in addition to markets and hierarchies (Ouchi 1980). Clan organizations have been studied in classic sociology as a particular, distinct type of social and economic institution (Durkheim 1893). They can be conceived also as mechanisms of social control that can be present either inside a hierarchical institution or in a market to generate hybrid forms of transaction governance (Ouchi 1979; Barney and Ouchi 1983). In general, a clan can be conceived of as a set of control mechanisms that are legitimated by "a high degree of goal congruence, typically through relatively complete socialization brought about through high inclusion" (Ouchi 1980: 136).

Clans are maintained by socially accepted norms of behavior, as contrasted with the formal rules of hierarchies and the market price system. The reconciliation of conflicting interests is achieved through generalized expectation of long-term, serial equilibrium among the contributions of all the participants to a given set of recurrent transactions. For clan members short-term disequilibria are acceptable among the investments that each part makes in the transaction because members can trust that other parties will obey the socially accepted reciprocity norm in the future. This property of serial equity of clans (Butler and Carney 1983) is contrasted with the instant equilibrium of parties' contributions obtained by markets and with the prerogatives of a central authority to resolve conflicts by imposition typical of hierarchies. The comparative properties of markets, bureaucracies, and clans in conflict resolution and in information processing have been summarized by Ouchi (1980) as in Table 2-1.

The concept of clan has its origins in the study of major social institutions that use social control mechanisms, such as churches, political parties, mutual benefit associations, and so on (Etzioni 1965; Selznick 1949; Lipset, Trow and Coleman 1956). The concept of clan was first applied by Ouchi to the study of business firms, especially in order to explain the Japanese miracle. The success of Japanese firms has been attributed to, among other things, a work atmosphere that is more trustful than the climate that exists in work organizations in western countries (Ouchi and Jaeger 1978; Ouchi 1981).

Table 2-1. Information Requirements and Conflict Resolution Properties of Markets, Bureaucracies, and Clans.

Mode of Control	Conflict Resolution Requirements	Informational Requirements
Market	• Instant reciprocity	Prices
Bureaucracy	• Reciprocity • Legitimate authority	Rules
Clans	• Serial reciprocity • Legitimate authority • Common values and beliefs	Traditions

Source: Adapted from Ouchi (1980).

Its marriage with the new institutional economics of Williamson has drawn more theoretical attention to the concept of clans as a form of control in business organizations. Williamson and Ouchi (1981) argue that, under conditions of extreme uncertainty and specificity of the transactions, both markets and bureaucracies will fail, and the clan form, which relies on goal congruence, becomes a superior way to regulate transactions. This happens when an exchanged good or service is highly innovative, ambiguous, and uncertain (which often occurs, for example, in highly professional services), so that it is difficult to anticipate its form and content and to measure not only its economic value but also its results. Under these conditions, both price systems and bureaucratic systems are not able to effectively control behaviors, productivity, or results (Ouchi 1979).

Hierarchical controls are useful when there is only moderate ambiguity in the measurement of performance. For example, Alchian and Demsetz (1972) demonstrate that a central agent (having residual rights on final total output) would be more efficient than a market mechanism in coordinating a production team in which each member's individual contribution to total output is undistinguishable and interdependent. However, the effectiveness of hierarchical direct control over behaviors, which makes it superior to market, decreases as task complexity increases. Alchian and Demsetz (1972) illustrate this problem with a case in which bureaucratic control becomes inefficient because the content of activities is so complex that the controller would almost have to execute the task himself in order to detect eventual elusive behaviors of the collaborator. In business firms there are many complex tasks for which performance is difficult to measure, such as basic R&D activities and several managerial activities. In these situations, social control is more efficient than bureaucratic control, taking into account that in these situations the exact measurement and monitoring of performances would not offset its costs and would produce biased behaviors. The clan form economizes on control costs when performance evaluation is highly ambiguous.

For clans to exercise effective social control, there must be systems for creating and maintaining a high degree of congruence among the members' goals (Ouchi 1980). Thus, clans need, and rely on, *a priori* processes of training, socialization, and cultural initiation instead of *a posteriori* managerial control. For the clan form these are some of the intrinsic transaction costs. However, relative to bureaucracies, the clan's costs are spent in conflict prevention rather than in conflict resolution. Consequently, the clan form will fail where the cost of maintaining a high degree of organizational inclusion and of identification with its goals (1) exceeds organizational resources or (2) is greater than the cost of tolerating elusion under the bureaucratic form.

Hierarchies and clans can be seen as two alternative organizational strategies for responding to market failure in conditions of high uncertainty and high conflict among interests. The hierarchical solution is designed to reduce uncertainty through the legitimate acquisition of information about other parties' behaviors, assuming that conflict of interest can hardly be reduced. By contrast, the clan solution is intended to reduce conflict among objectives through intense socialization, assuming that task complexity prevents the reduction of uncertainty. One implication of comparing hierarchies and clans in this way is that there is an impossibility zone, defined by high conflict of interest *and* high information ambiguity. As Barney and Ouchi (1983) have pointed out, no transaction is likely to take place in such situations.

What are the effects when clan mechanisms are applied "to assist" a hierarchical or a market form? Other things being equal, the addition of clan mechanisms enhances the capacity to regulate more complex transactions. This shifts hierarchy toward an organic mixed organizational form and markets toward a managed market.

Williamson (1970) has analytically demonstrated this hypothesis as to hierarchies; Japanese firms are an example of this possibility. If the rate of compliance is higher, there is the possibility of maintaining efficient structures of larger size because of the reduction of internal control loss and discretionary behaviors costs.

Regarding managed markets (Butler and Carney 1983), let us suppose that a complex transaction (such as the sale of chemical manufacturing equipment or sophisticated aircraft) is to be regulated through market exchange for reasons of economies of specialization and scale and because the low frequency of the transaction does not justify the cost of an internal structure. The efficiency of the exchange process can be decisively augmented if a trust atmosphere exists and long-term relationships are nurtured by reciprocal favors (Barney and Ouchi 1983). Grafting the clan mechanism to the market form allows its effective performance beyond the conditions required for its survival as a pure form.

48	PERSPECTIVES ON ORGANIZATION THEORY

This analysis of Ouchi's extension of OFF suggests two strengths that the current version of M&H has over its earlier formulations. First, it has been useful to describe or define the degree of conflict among the actor's interests as a *variable* and not an endemic fixed condition. Economic actors' propensity to opportunism will then vary not only depending on (1) uncertainty and substitutability but also depending on (2) the degree of conflict in the structure of the games they are playing, and most of all, on (3) the expected duration (repetitions) of the game.[14] By considering the state of conflict among actors' objectives, an interesting part of Williamson's residual, ad hoc construct of atmosphere, is brought into the analytically specified part of OFF.[15]

Second, many business experiences can be explained by accounting for goal congruence and clan mechanisms. They are cases in which a highly integrated and traditional national culture enhances compliance and also in which particular proprietary arrangements enhance goal congruence—as, for example, in cooperative firms.

Third, the current extended version of comparative institutional analysis has improved its capacity to explain, in terms of relative efficiency, both the pure forms of organization and those mixed forms that have attracted the attention of businesspersons and scholars. A realistic comparison of alternative organizational forms could not, in fact, omit the evaluation of a continuum of hybrid forms such as decentralized organic internal structures (Lawrence and Dyer 1983), quasi-firms generated by the modern forms of production externalization (Eccles 1981), quasi-market mechanisms operating inside M-form hierarchies (Chandler 1977), franchising agreements (Rubin 1978), and solidaristic interfirm associations (Zan 1982).

Technology and Power: Are They Rival Explanations?

Small numbers and uncertainty are not the sole determinants of efficient organizational structures. They are the main factors in comparative analysis of production and transaction costs. But this does not mean that it is impossible to study how major changes in other context variables can shift the general level of transaction and production costs under different forms of governance (small numbers and uncertainty being equal). Some of the other variables that play this role in OFF have been discussed earlier. They are, for example, the degree of congruence among objectives and organizational culture (Ouchi 1979, 1980), the frequency at which a given transaction occurs (Williamson 1981; Daems 1983), and the expected longevity of the relationships (Barney and Ouchi 1983).

Two other important exogenous variables that can affect the level of production and transaction costs, regardless of the states assumed by uncertainty and substitutability, are technology and power. Jones's work (1982) has focused on the role that technology, as contrasted with transaction costs, plays in determining the internalization of production that characterized the passage from the putting-out system to the factory system in the eighteenth century. Actually, Williamson (1983) and Jones differ in how they estimate the weight of these two different variables in determining that particular historical event of hierarchy formation rather than on more theoretical grounds. In fact, no elaboration in the M&H perspective asserts that, in general, *exogenous* technological shocks that affect transaction and production costs should have less weight in explaining efficient organization structures, with respect to *intrinsic* differences among the various structures' costs. Williamson's emphasis on the relevance of transactions costs is a matter of presentation and stems from the targets that he usually addresses. It should not be confused with the general propositions of his model.

Several works, in fact, are similar to the M&H perspective and pay particular attention to how major technological transformations have affected production and transaction costs and the comparative efficiency of organization structures (Chandler 1977). There are also other analyses of the effect of technology on efficient organizational solutions in M&H or similar views. First, technology obviously affects technical indivisibility among work-flow stations and then the size of the firm technological core (Williamson 1981).[16] Another important way in which technology affects comparative organization efficiency is through task ambiguity and the difficulty of performance measurement (Alchian and Demsetz 1972). In this case, highly ambiguous technologies rule out both purely bureaucratic forms and market relationships to the advantage of mixed, clan-assisted forms (Barney and Ouchi 1983). Another example, not well developed but worth some theoretical and empirical work, is the role of information systems technology in making some hierarchical or quasi-market structures feasible or more efficient.[17]

The most lively debate about rival variables to transaction costs is about the role of power. The M&H perspective has been criticized because it neglects power objectives as a determinant of organizational arrangements (Perrow 1981; Bauer and Cohen 1983; Francis 1983). This criticism applies to both interorganizational and intraorganizational relations. In the case of interorganizational relations, it has been argued that mergers, joint ventures, associations, or other mixed forms of interorganizational coordination are best explained by a motive of control over scarce critical resources on which firms depend (Pfeffer and Salancik 1978). With respect to internal organization, it has been shown that social actors orient their organizational choices toward increasing the amount of discretionary slack resources and reducing their dependence and substitutability (Crozier and Friedberg 1977; Pfeffer and Salancik 1978).

The debate about the role of power arises for different reasons. Pfeffer (1982) suggests that the rival hypotheses of efficiency and power as determinants of organizational structures must be resolved through empirical research. Perrow (1981) sees the issue in terms of an ideological choice between the interests of different social actors: If I am to be commanded, controlled, or fiated, I would prefer bargaining, written guarantees, a legal statement of rights and obligations, and in general the ability to act as an autonomous agent, no matter what the transaction costs.

There is another way to approach this power issue. The power argument can be divided in two conceptual parts. One part of the argument asserts in effect, although in a different language, that transaction costs can be unequally distributed so that different preference orderings over organizational arrangements should be, in general, expected. Both in the case of interfirm and in the case of interindividual or group relationships, the transaction cost for one actor can be assigned positive preferences by the counterpart and vice versa. Also, more simply, different actors may give different weights to various categories of transaction costs so that the overall ranking of possible organizational solutions is different for the two parties. In this respect, the power argument indicates a need to expand, rather than reject, the transaction-cost approach. In its present version, organizational decisionmakers are implicitly assumed to be a team (in the sense of information economics) with homogeneous preferences over organizational alternatives. Given the range and relevance of the phenomena that OFF seeks to explain, it should however adopt a more realistic posture regarding multiple preferences. This point will be elaborated in Chapter 3, which draws from earlier work by Williamson (1964, 1970).

The second component of the power argument requires a step beyond the transaction-cost approach. Trouble arises when two parties to a transaction are neither perfectly substitutable or locked in idiosyncratic interdependence but are in conditions of asymmetrical dependence. In other words, one party is less substitutable of the other or dominates the other. In such cases, not only will the parties prefer to regulate their relationship differently, but also one party has a greater probability of attaining its preferred solution. In these situations, it is not possible to (1) predict or prescribe any single particular organizational arrangement with the *sole* criterion of efficiency or (2) consider only transaction-cost reduction objectives. A realistic theoretical framework should then consider the reduction of dependence and the control over resources as objectives or independent variables. Chapter 3 analyzes the valence, in terms of dependence reduction, of a full continuum of interorganizational arrangements.

NOTES

1. More formally, if a group is a team, the preference ordering of the group always satisfies all these conditions: It obeys the transitivity property and the Pareto optimality principle; it is complete with respect to all the state of the world considered in the individual orderings; it satisfies the rule of unanimity of all the individuals in ordering all the state of the world that they consider (Marschak 1954).
2. For example:

Levels of Output
(Production Department's choice)

		O1	O2	O3
	P1	0	2	5
Prices (Sales Department's choice)	P2	2	3	2
	P3	10	6	1

The numbers in the cells indicate the level of utility for both departments because, by definition, in a team all players have common preferences.

3. The number of individuals who respond directly and hierarchically to the same supervisor.

4. The profit expression is constructed as follows. The maximized difference is $R - C$ (revenue minus costs). $R = PQ$, where P is unit price and Q is total output. $C = \sum_{i=1}^{n} w_i N_i + rQ$, where w_i is salary at the ith hierarchical level, N_i is the number of employees at the ith level, and r are all nonwage variable costs per unit of output. The level of output Q is then expressed as $Q = (\alpha S)^{n-1}$, which is a function (for simplicity considered equal to 1) of the rate of compliance of individuals toward orders α, multiplied by the number of individuals under each supervisor, raised to the $n - 1$ power—that is, the number of passages that communications and orders must do along the hierarchical levels. If we also express $w_i N_i$ as a function of the wage w_0 at the lower level and of the rate of interlevel salary differentiation β, we have

$$R - C = PQ - \sum_{i=1}^{n} w_i N_i - rQ = P(\alpha s)^{n-1} - \sum_{i=1}^{n} w_0 \, \beta^{n-1} s^{i-1} - r(\alpha s)^{n-1}$$

5. Expositions of the main market failure factors are offered by Bator (1958) and Marschak (1965).

6. Williamson (1975) discusses the extent to which various forms of adaptive contracting are capable of resolving uncertainty. For example, he considers contingent claim contracts (in which different solutions are contemplated depending on the occurrence of different possible external events) and other forms of long-term contracting in which many aspects of the agreement are left open to future negotiations on the occurrence of uncertain events (such as sequential spot contracting).

7. The author's main reference here is to the analyses of opportunistic, strategic behavior by Goffman (1969) and Schelling (1960).

8. This might be perceived as a drawback of the new perspective, but it can be—and in my opinion should be—seen as a strength. In fact, rather than being juxtaposed with no relation with existing theories, the transaction-cost approach to internal organization helps explain some of the *whys* of the previous contingency theory and is consistent with some well-documented empirical tendencies of organization shown by that paradigm. Consistency with well-founded theoretical models of internal organization is a desirable property of a model that has been mainly developed to explain external organization.

9. Other authors, who have recently contributed to the M&H perspective are J. Barney, W. Ouchi, R. Eccles, R. Burton, B. Obel, E. Anderson, B. Weitz, and D. Teece. Related views are those of A. Chandler, A. Hirschman, and C. Lindblom. For a comprehensive picture of contributions in the M&H and related perspectives, see R.C.D. Nacamulli, A. Rugiadini, eds, *Organizzazione e mercato* (Bologna: Il Mulino, 1985).

10. See the first section of this chapter and Williamson (1970).

11. The notion of an elementary scheme has been used in the major evolutionary models of organizations (Chandler 1962; Scott 1971). On simple structures see also Williamson (1970, 1975).

12. Williamson (1964) has labeled this phenomenon *discretionary behavior.* See also the first section of Chapter 3.

13. A corrupted multidivisional form is defined as a structure in which top management is involved in operating decisions and divisions are not autonomous, self-contained quasi-firms that are evaluated on—and therefore are oriented to—profit global results (Williamson 1975: 153).

14. These hypotheses are in fact consistent with game theory indications (Axelrod 1984).

15. In presenting the four basic explanatory variables of organizational failure events (uncertainty, small numbers, bounded rationality, and opportunism) Williamson (1975) specifies that the actual level of "information impactedness" generated by them also depends on the prevailing cultural attitudes toward the different modes of control and on the customs regarding trust. All of these variables—defining the cultural context on which a transaction takes place—are grouped into the background, somehow ad hoc category of "atmosphere."

16. For example, the technical feasibility of internal and external organizational arrangements are more varied in mechanical industry than in chemical industry because of a greater technical divisibility of production processes in the former.

17. An example here is the diffusion in the tourism industry of forms of vertical and horizontal quasi-integration (such as holdings, federations or franchising systems, grouping tour operators, hotel chains, transportation companies, and so forth) supported by computerized real-time booking systems.

3 ORGANIZATION DESIGN WITH MULTIPLE OBJECTIVES

In the economic approach to business organizations presented in Chapter 2, organizational solutions are evaluated and chosen with a single objective—profitability. In the approaches examined in Chapter 3, it is assumed that more benevolent environmental conditions allow the firm to pursue a wider set of objectives—profitability plus power plus, eventually, other goals.

The assumptions about the firm's preference function are further expanded in the models discussed in this chapter. Conflict among the preference functions of different interdependent firms will govern decisions about how to organize their relationships.

A third way in which the domain of the models in this chapter is wider than those considered earlier is that it treats conditions of asymmetrical dependence. In other words, there can be different weights assigned to the various parties' preferences—that is, power can be unequally distributed.

Two theories are considered in this section: (1) Williamson's (1964, 1970) economics of discretionary behavior (reconsidered as a theory of the effective multiple objectives organization) and (2) the power seeking firm of the resource dependence perspective (Pfeffer and Salancik 1978). In the last part of the chapter, a comparison of the two theories refutes the common opinion that they are rival theories.

ORGANIZATIONAL FAILURES WITH
MULTIPLE OBJECTIVES

Williamson's (1964) initial idea was to bridge organizational theories of individual managerial needs and motives with economic analysis, bringing them to bear on the theory of the firm and economic organization. He translated the basic individual needs analyzed in organizational behavior into economic variables. The variables he has defined may be seen as means to attain those human goals. Managers' motives such as salary, security, status, power, prestige, and professional excellence have found their economic translation in the notion of expense preference. Williamson (1964: 33) explains that "Managers do not have a neutral attitude toward all classes of expenses. Instead, some types of expenses have positive values attached to them."

There are three main types of positively valued expenses. One category is the positive managerial expense preference for staff. Managers prefer to expand personnel and hierarchical expenses of their own departments as a means of satisfying power, security, and salary needs and professional group interests. A second category of pursued expenses is slack resources, in terms of emoluments (incentives beyond the equilibrium levels requested to retain individuals' contributions) and on-the-job leisure (discretionary time and unallocated energy). A third type of managerial objective is the discretionary or slack profit that can be appropriated once stockholders have been allowed a minimum acceptable profit level.

This is a substantially wider version of the basic information economics model that Williamson (1970) elaborated to determine the limits to firm size (see Chapter 2). As Williamson argues (1964, 1970) in the case of competition among many firms and low barriers to industry entry there may be little room for discretionary behavior. But when the environment is permissive or munificent, the accumulation of slack resources may be a large-scale phenomenon.

Which consequences of firm utility functions include resource control objectives on the efficient organizational boundaries? Williamson's analysis leads to a conclusion that matches our intuitive judgment: Optimal organizational boundaries are wider when managerial objectives enter the utility function than in the case of pure transaction costs minimization.[1]

The next step is to model organizational choice when the actors' preferences are not homogeneous. In fact, in the basic model of discretionary behavior (outlined in note 1), it is still assumed that the firm utility function, although including power and other objectives, is unitary, or commonly shared by the firm's managers. Williamson (1964) has elaborated a modified version of the model that integrates social choice. He starts with a discussion of Arrow's (1951) impossibility theorem, which addresses the difficulties of integrating different individual preference orderings in a group ordering. Williamson assumes that these difficulties are irrelevant in an institutional context. When actors belong to the same institution, some agreement is likely to emerge about a procedure for integrating individual preferences. Some bounds are also posed by organizational culture on the variations in individual preferences. This premise opens the path to an analytical treatment of the multiple actor, multiple preference choice of organizational structure. The model uses Marschak's (1954) notion of a foundation to distinguish (1) the case of a group of individuals who have *different* preference orderings over organizational solutions from (2) the case of a team (in which a condition of unanimity is satisfied). The overall utility function maximized by a firm, conceived as a foundation, then, includes an individual utility function for each different manager (or interest center), taking the following form: Max $W = W(U_1, U_2, \ldots, U_n)$, where $1, 2, \ldots, n$, are the different managers or subunits. Each individual utility function is the inclusive of the range of objectives already mentioned for the unitary utility function model.[2] The optimal organizational solution is expressed, as in the unitary model, through the principal decision variable of optimal boundaries, or organization size. In the foundation case, however, differently from the team case, a substantive solution about optimal boundaries cannot be calculated. The solution will, in fact, depend on two important contingency factors: (1) the weight of each manager's preference within the firm ($\frac{\partial W}{\partial U_i}$) and (2) the intensity of each manager's preferences for each of his objectives ($\frac{\partial U_i}{\partial Y_j}$).

An important point worth stressing about managerial discretionary behavior theory is that in the case of multiple preferences it has been necessary to introduce a power variable into the model. In fact, as

Williamson (1964) illustrates (by quoting Horwicz 1956), "the weight assigned to any member's desire may be viewed as that member's legitimate power in the group."

A question was left open in these early elaborations by Williamson on the multiple preference problem. The approach of the economics of discretionary behavior applies to the case of multiple preferences, under the assumption that potential conflict of interests is reduced by belonging to the same institutional context (Williamson 1964). If the approach is applied to the collective choice of an *interfirm* organizational structure, this assumption cannot be safely accepted. Therefore, it is necessary to further relax the assumption about the preference function of the group of economic actors involved in the organizational decision. The notion of a coalition is useful for this purpose (Marschak 1954; Cyert and March 1963). It is, in terms of its preferences' structure, a third type of group in addition to the rational team and foundation. The preference structure that defines a coalition is not necessarily required to satisfy either a unanimity condition (as a team does) or to have a weighting system that allows the comparison and integration of preferences (as a foundation). For this case of coalition, negotiation is the only mechanism that can narrow the distance among different actors' preferences. As observed, the question of how a coalition can reach an agreement about an effective organizational structure has been left open in transaction costs reduction views as well as in resource dependence reduction views, as we shall see. This problem will be discussed in Chapter 7.

THE RESOURCE DEPENDENCE PERSPECTIVE

Basic Assumptions

The important effect of the creation of interfirm organizational (rather than market) linkages is *changing* the state of uncertainty and the number of firms involved in a given array of transactions. In particular, the establishment of a hierarchy to govern a broad array of transactions, as in the case of a merger, will, *inter alia*, involve *changes in small-number conditions* in the merged firms' external transactional environment. It is therefore not unrealistic to assume that firms evaluate, according to their own preference, such effects of their decisions on the configuration of their interorganizational links. Under any circumstances one can assume that these preferences about the states of environment favor a more benevolent or permissive environment rather than a less favorable or more constrained one.

It follows that the firm utility function includes positive preferences for slack profits (such as monopoly profit), as well as for the accumulation of slack physical and human resources. Therefore, where possible, firms will adopt strategies aimed at altering their environment in order to gain these advantages. The proponents of the resource dependence perspective advanced by Pfeffer and Salancik (1978) express this assumption by postulating the existence of a firm objective to reduce dependence on external factors, that is the principal determinant in the choice of interorganizational arrangement. Resource dependence is defined as follows:

> Concentration of the control of discretion over resources and the importance of the resources to the organization together determine the focal organization's dependence on any given other group or organization. Dependence can then be defined as the product of the importance of a given input or output to the organization and the extent to which it is controlled by a relatively few organizations (Pfeffer and Salancik 1978: 51).

Resource dependence used this way can be linked to the economic notions of substitutability of both the sources from which the firm's inputs derive and also the resources themselves.

A second aspect of resource dependence is that a firm (or other institution) may be the source of the focal firm's resources because it owns these resources or because it is entitled of exclusive control over them. Control of resources is in itself a variable representing the relative capacity of one actor, vis-à-vis other actors, to determine the allocation or use of such resources. The capacity of discretionary use that a firm has over resources defines its degree of control.

Pfeffer and Salancik draw their notion of control over, or dependence on, resources from both sociological and economic analyses of decisionmaking processes in firms that weigh the aggregate capacity of several actors to exert influence rather than merely their relative irreplaceability. In fact, first, Pfeffer and Salancik take into account the research on the sociology of organizations involving the analysis of power and the strategies needed to gain and maintain it (Emerson 1962; Blau 1964; Crozier 1963). Second, they include economic approaches to dependence (Jacobs 1974). Third, they make use of the notion that the market does, in fact, operate in many situations (particularly small-number situations) through social mechanisms. It thus becomes possible to apply social dynamics analysis tools such as role theory to corporate behavior, in the sense that the behavior of each firm will tend to be constrained by the overall role expectations of all the other organizations with which it is in direct contact—such as suppliers, consumers, distributors, unions, government bodies, and so forth (Evan 1966).

With this eclectic approach, Pfeffer and Salancik highlight and analyze interfirm organizational strategies aimed at exerting influence (such as tacit or informal cooperation, social norms, associations, cartels, interlocking directorates, and joint ventures) as complementary or alternative to strategies aimed at changing the boundaries of firms[3] in the strict sense—that is, mergers and acquisitions. Their main hypotheses and research findings on the various possible organizational responses to various degrees and configurations of external control are discussed in the following section.

Dependence and Changes in
Organizational Boundaries

A firm's scope for action will depend on a variety of relationships with external actors (such as competing firms, suppliers, customers, banks, and public agencies) that may have well-defined expectations and preferences regarding the behavior of the firm concerned.

The classic response in structural organizational theory is that the firm adapts to demands on it that come from the outside. In terms of organizational arrangements, this implies adopting internal structures and mechanisms that are fit to such demands. As Pfeffer and Salancik note, however, this is not the only kind of response possible. Actually, a firm must adapt in situations in which it is not feasible (1) to evade the demands or (2) alter the environment.

Evading environmental demands has been analyzed in organizational theory as uncertainty avoidance and quasi-resolution of conflict (March and Simon 1958; Cyert and March 1963; Galbraith 1973, 1977). Examples of these behaviors are the reduction in levels of aspiration relating to the firm's performance, and the sequential allocation of managerial effort over time to satisfy demands that conflict with each other. The response of changing the environment has, however, been neglected in the traditional notion of the organization as an information-processing system. Pfeffer (1972) and Pfeffer and Salancik (1978) have concentrated their attention on this second strategy. Indeed, the adoption of strategies aimed at modifying the environment implies that the firm not only processes information but also controls resources, which can be used in offering rewards, issuing sanctions, and making promises and threats. Pfeffer and Salancik divide organizational strategies aimed at changing the environment into two categories:

1. Strategies that involve changes of ownership—that is, the transfer under the governance of a single firm of relationships that previously existed between different firms. These strategies are called alteration of the environment. Examples are diversification, vertical integration (between industries), and horizontal integration (within industries);

2. Strategies that do not involve mergers or acquisitions but the creation of quasi-hierarchical relations—such as joint ventures, interlocking boards of directors, associations, and cartels—and the formation of social norms to regulate corporate behavior. These strategies make the firms' environment a negotiated environment.

A second major point raised by Pfeffer and Salancik relates to the type of dependence that such strategies can resolve. Two (or more) firms may be interdependent because the output of one is the input of the other. This interdependence, arising from the exchange of goods or services (that is, transactions) is here defined as *transactional* (the term used by Pfeffer and Salancik is *symbiotic*, which they derived from resource dependence analysis in biology). Firms may also be interdependent because their survival and success depend on the same resources. Because the interdependence here is based on the distribution of the same resources, it is called *competitive interdependence*.

Another aspect of the concept of dependence is that interfirm dependence relationships, instead of being *reciprocal* (interdependence), can be *asymmetric* (unilateral dependence) (Pfeffer and Salancik 1978: 52–53). These distinctions are of fundamental importance if one is to understand that the sources both of market failures and also of the creation of organizational coordination mechanisms (of both a hierarchical and nonhierarchical nature) do not merely turn on issues of transactional interdependence. It is well known in theories of games and collective choice that hierarchies and other mechanisms of organizational control can be required to solve competitive interdependence situations that are insoluble if players behave as unilateral utility maximizers (Arrow 1951, 1974).

Furthermore, these distinctions are necessary to understand that a state asymmetric dependence will foster the creation of a hierarchy external to the focal relationships, where it is not possible to absorb or influence directly the source of dependence. For instance, asymmetric dependence explains the association of dependent firms in organizational networks that enable a countervailing power (Galbraith 1952; Pfeffer and Salancik 1978: 52) to be set against that of the dominant firm. Asymmetrical dependence, coupled with a dependence reduction objective, also explains strategies aimed at increasing the sources of resources in order to reduce the firm's overall dependence on external factors (such as diversification strategies).

Research on Mergers. The study of dependence between firms covers the relationships between firms belonging to different industries as well as between firms within the same industry. The measurement of interindustry interdependence is intended to assess transactional interdependence between clusters of firms that have input/ output relationships at the national economic system level, on the assumption that it is a good predictor of vertical integration strategies (or of other interindustry organizational coordination forms). To identify this interdependence, transactions derived from Leontief input/output matrices (1966), relative to U.S. economy, were used. The principal variables considered were the proportion of output from each industry i sold to each industry j; the proportion of the input of each industry acquired by each other industry; and the proportion of the total input and output transactions of each industry with each other industry (Pfeffer and Salancik 1978: 116).

The interdependence between firms within each industry was measured in a similar way, on the assumption that it could explain the differences between industries by horizontal integration and other forms of industry organization. As we shall shortly show, the best predictors of industry internal organization are different than predictors for interindustry organization.

Within an industry, organization can be better explained by the degree of competitive interdependence rather than by the degree of transactional interdependence. The measurement of competitive interdependence used by Pfeffer and Salancik is based on the hypothesis that such interdependence is related to the number of firms in the industry. In this regard, the authors (Pfeffer and Salancik 1978: 124) accept the proposition, derived from economic theory and research (Stern and Morgenroth 1968; Stigler 1974), that

> uncertainty is curvilinearly related to industrial concentration, in an inverted U-shaped relationship. When there are many firms in an industry and concentration is relatively low, the actions of any firm represent only a small proportion of the total industry; thus, any firm has few consequential effects on most of the other firms. As concentration increases, an oligopolistic market structure is reached, in which firms have increasing impact on each other. As concentration increases even more, uncertainty begins to decrease. With only a very few large firms operating, tacit coordination becomes possible, and each develops stable expectations concerning the others' behavior.

Vertical Integration. On the basis of statistical sources and economic reports on mergers and on exchanges between manufacturing industries, Pfeffer (1972) and Pfeffer and Salancik (1978) have found a significant correlation between mergers M_{ij} (the percentage of mergers between companies in industry i with companies in industry j)[4] and all three indicators of transactional dependence used (S_{ij} = percentage of industry i's sales made to industry j; P_{ij} = percentage of industry i's purchases made from industry j; and T_{ij} = percentage of total transactions of industry i made with industry j). Among the control variables, considered as possible alternative explanations for mergers, it is interesting to note that the rates of profitability and the rates of concentration of industries j, which are supposed to explain entry into new industries according to standard economic theory, were not correlated to the mergers actually observed.

Moreover—to test the hypothesis that mergers are effected with the motive of reducing dependence, and not for other reasons—the authors make specific hypotheses about the direction in which vertical integration would occur if it were being carried out to reduce dependence.[5] They argue that the firm's dependence on its customers may differ from its dependence on its suppliers and hypothesize that integration will occur in the direction in which the firm is facing the most uncertain interdependencies. Two specific propositions were tested and supported by the data (Pfeffer and Salancik 1978: 121–22):

1. That the correlation between mergers (M_{ij}) and interdependence in purchase transactions (P_{ij}) will be greater in more highly concentrated industries, in which buyers have few alternatives and therefore do not have to cope with any particular difficulties on the sales side; and

2. That the correlation between mergers (M_{ij}) and interdependence in sales transactions (S_{ij}) will be higher in industries with an intermediate level of concentration, in which the uncertainty due to competition is greater both with respect to situations of high concentration (where there is high market power) and with respect to situations that are close to perfect competition (where there is low strategic interaction uncertainty).

Horizontal Integration.   The correlation between transactional interdependence within industries and the number of mergers is weak.[6] The authors thus hypothesize that the principal variable explaining intraindustry mergers is uncertainty arising from competitive interdependence. According to the hypothesis that this kind of uncertainty is linked by a reverse U-curve with the rate of concentration in the industry (see above), one would expect the number of mergers to reach a peak in industries with an intermediate rate of concentration. This hypothesis is supported by data (Pfeffer and Salancik 1978: 125). Therefore the authors can conclude that the individual variable that best explains vertical integration strategies is transactional cross-industry interdependence, while horizontal integration is best explained by competitive within-industry interdependence..

However, these variables explain only part of the variance in dependent variables M_{ij} and M_{ii} (that is, the number of cross-industry mergers and intraindustry mergers.[7] The authors therefore consider a third type of mergers, which derives not from integration strategies but from diversification strategies.

Diversification.   The hypothesis is that corporate acquisitions due to diversification decisions take place in different directions from those driven by greater transactional and competitive interdependence. This hypothesis is based on the premise that diversification is an alternative to integration in reducing dependence where, for some reason, integration is not feasible. As Pfeffer and Salancik (1978: 127) state, "Diversification is a way of avoiding the *domination* that comes from *asymmetric exchanges* when *it is not possible to absorb* or in some other way gain increased control over the powerful external exchange partners."

There may be a variety of reasons for barriers to integration between interdependent firms. For instance, the industry representing the firm's market outlet may be highly concentrated, while in the focal industry horizontal integration aimed at establishing a countervailing power may be difficult due to differences in legislation, in policies, in organizational culture, and so forth. An extreme case of this, cited by the authors, is represented by firms that sell most of their products to the government. Indeed, in the case of the United States, using the findings of one of the largest surveys on U.S. diversification (Gort 1962), Pfeffer and Salancik demonstrate that as the proportion of a firm's revenue with the federal government increases, so does the likelihood that the firm will seek to diversify. Again, one might well deduce from the explanation of diversification provided by the RD theory that, *ceteris paribus*, firms producing commodities will have greater incentives to diversify than firms producing industrial goods because they cannot develop tight control mechanisms over their market outlets. A final motive that can make a diversification strategy rise in a firm's preference order, with respect to alternative integration strategies, is that a firm takes into account the expected increase in its transaction costs where its own integration strategy is likely to provoke countervailing power moves in interdependent industries.

If these are the motives behind diversification, resource dependence relationships should not be particularly helpful in predicting the *direction* that mergers due to diversification, as opposed to integration, are likely to take. Indeed, Pfeffer and Salancik themselves hypothesize that, in the diversification case, firms are not constrained to follow their own existing interdependence relationships in selecting potential acquisition targets. It is reasonable to hypothesize that the decisions to diversify may be more strongly based on the profitability of the target companies than in the integration case. This hypothesis was tested and supported by the analysis of the distributions for profitability of companies acquired (1) for vertical and horizontal integration purposes and (2) for product diversification

Figure 3-1. Relationships between Change in Organizational Boundaries and Types of Interfirm Interdependence.

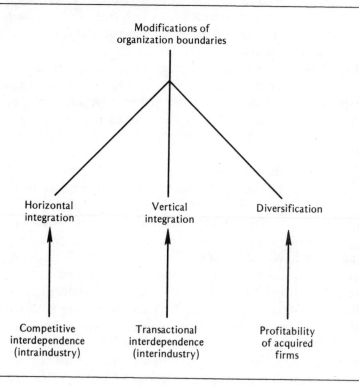

purposes (Pfeffer and Salancik 1978: 134). To sum up, Pfeffer and Salancik's findings on the changing of organizational boundaries allow three types of boundary modification strategies to be related with the three explanatory variables that are most closely correlated with them, as shown in the diagram in Figure 3-1.[8]

Dependence and Coordination Mechanisms between Firms

Organizations coordinate in many ways—cooptation, trade associations, cartels, reciprocal trade agreements, coordinating councils, advisory boards, boards of directors, joint ventures, and social norms. Each represents a way of sharing power and a social agreement which stabilizes and coordinates *mutual interdependence.* Such strategies are much more common than total absorption, as in merger, and are particularly useful when coordination is needed only occasionally. Organizations that need occasional access to the capital markets do not need to own or control financial institutions. Rather, what they need are assurances of support and capital when it is required. In other circumstances, coordination is achieved *more readily*, when accomplished through a central coordinating organization. If there are many small competitors, merger, or acquisition, to substantially concentrate the industry is not feasible. Under such conditions, the development of strong business associations, such as the various farmer organizations or professional associations, is more likely.

Coordination has the advantage of being *more flexible* than managing dependence through ownership. Relationships established through communication and consensus can be established, renegotiated, and reestablished with more ease than the integration of organizations by merger can be altered. The disadvantage of this less complete absorption of interdependence is the *less than absolute control* it provides over the other organizations. Interdependence is a situation in which another has the discretion to take actions which affect the focal organization's interests. For the organizations seeking greater autonomy, the critical task is how to reduce the other's discretion and simultaneously align it with the focal organization's own interests. The problem is how to coordinate the other's actions so that they are compatible with what the focal organization wants. *Ownership solves* the problem directly; compliance comes *through the authority* established by owning the other organization. Coordination through interfirm linkages depends on voluntary behavior; significant discretion remains with external organizations who may withdraw from the coordinated interaction (Pfeffer and Salancik 1978: 144–45, italics added).

This lengthy quote from Pfeffer and Salancik (1978) suggests the variety of variables that may determine the superiority of strategies aimed at establishing interfirm coordination mechanisms over strategies aimed at changing interfirm boundaries. It also suggests that these variables have not been dealt with systematically by the RD perspective. However, on the basis of research findings and on the economic and sociological models on which they are based, it is possible to identify the following explanatory variables.

Cooperative Games. In the terms of game theory, a prerequisite for the existence of space for organizational coordination is that the firm-players can achieve the same or better results through agreement than by acting on their own. This means that the game has to have a cooperative element—that is, parties must have some common interests. The organizationally relevant proposition that follows from this game theory theorem is that when these common interests are strong and are clearly perceived, tacit coordination can be successfully used and complex formal integration mechanisms are less necessary. Therefore, highly interdependent firms need not merge or develop complicated control mechanisms as long as the opportunism potential of the relation is low because of the structure of payoffs.

Unilateral Dependence.   The above discussion refers to a case of equal power distribution. Unilateral dependence can be another reason that, in addition to cooperativeness of the game structure, a quasi-market relation can survive between firms linked by high resource interdependence. In this case complex bureaucratic guarantees and controls are substituted for imposition, and compliance is obtained by one party because the other has no alternative. These propositions are supported by some economic research findings cited by Pfeffer and Salancik (1978: 175-76) to describe the conditions in which associations, coalitions, and cartels of firms are formed. For example, Phillips (1960) studied the degree of formalization in interfirm coordination as a function of a set of independent variables. He found that, the number of firms to be coordinated being equal, the mechanisms needed were less formal when the distribution of power was more asymmetric and when the firm's objectives were more similar (the more cooperative the game).

Interaction Frequency.   This variable is based on the pure economics of information. If the structure of the game allows effective coordination mechanisms to emerge, more formal and more extensive mechanisms will be more costly. Accordingly, it will become economic to use them only at certain levels of interaction frequency, to which coordination can be applied to produce benefits. This variable—interaction frequency—is therefore used in RD theory much in the same way in which it is used in OFF (Daems 1983)—that is, to explain the formation of institutional arrangements that fall midway between market and hierarchy.

Barriers to Interfirm Integration.   Developing coordination mechanisms between firms, rather than obtaining integration by merger, may be the only available route where there are legal constraints or scarcity of resources that preclude concentration. First, legal or political barriers are factors that could make the cost of changing boundaries higher than the cost of interfirm nonhierarchical coordination. Second, owing to resource unavailability, the most preferred organizational arrangement—such as a merger with a scarcely substitutable supplier—could be unfeasible given the firm's size and financial resources, making interfirm coordination mechanisms the best alternative.

Uncertainty. Pfeffer and Salancik make the statement that under conditions where uncertainty is high, types of coordination other than hierarchy, associated with ownership, have advantages of flexibility. This is, however, a very particular aspect of the question.

Different coordination mechanisms can be distinguished in terms of their ability to cope with uncertainty. Indeed, social norms, one of the coordination mechanisms considered by RD, may in fact be more effective than hierarchy under high uncertainty conditions in which performances and results are difficult to predict and to measure (Ouchi 1980). In any case, the effectiveness of social control mechanisms is subject to the limitation that the norms of social behavior are based on a perception of common interests, whether they derive from the strictly cooperative nature of the game or from expectations of reciprocity and stability in the game.[9]

The effectiveness of *social* coordination mechanisms, thus, is contingent on conditions of both uncertainty and conflict of interest that must be distinguished from those in which *organizational* coordination mechanisms are effective—such as joint ventures, interlocking boards of directors, associations, and cartels.[10]

For the reasons illustrated above, and drawing from the Barney and Ouchi (1983) work on intermediate organizational forms, some reasonable hypotheses can be advanced about the comparative efficiency of social and bureaucratic interfirm coordination mechanisms. Social coordination—or "market assisted by clan," to use Barney and Ouchi's words—is more efficient when uncertainty is very high and conflict among objectives is low. Formal inter-organizational coordination— or "market assisted by bureaucracy"—is more efficient when uncertainty is less high and conflict of interest is relevant. In sum, formal interfirm coordination should be more convenient in intermediate conditions of uncertainty and conflict, social coordination in conditions of high uncertainty and low conflict.

The above propositions derive from considerations of transactions costs due to opportunism potential and should hold, other things being equal. The issue (raised by Pfeffer and Salancik) of the greater flexibility of intermediate forms with respect to mergers in the face of uncertainty seems to be justifiable in terms of the higher expected production and administrative costs of internal structure (rather than transaction costs) when the frequency of a given transaction varies in unpredictable ways. Then, externalization of the transaction may reduce expected costs acting as a buffer.

Pfeffer and Salancik's (1978) findings about joint venture activity do not contrast with these hypotheses. Their results show that joint ventures are used to resolve competitive interdependence, while mergers are used to regulate transactional interdependence, which is likely to be more complex to manage.[11]

Number of Firms. All interfirm linkages can be applied to two or more interdependent firms. As the number of firms to be coordinated rises, however, there will be a limit to the size that can be achieved by a network of organizational relationships. The reasons are analogous to the information and organization costs that constrain the size that can be reached by a hierarchy (Williamson 1970; see Chapter 2).

In fact, Pfeffer and Salancik (1978: 156) justify, on the basis of information costs, the hypothesis that there is an inverse relationship between the number of joint ventures and interlocking directorates on the one hand and the number of firms to be coordinated on the other:

> The ability of n number of organizations to communicate with each other decreases as the number of organizations increases. The number of links required to fully connect a network of n organizations is: $n(n-1)/2$. When two organizations are involved, only one interchange is necessary. With 10 organizations, 45 linkages must take place to connect the organizations fully. Thus, the feasibility of developing an interfirm organization is increased when there are fewer firms to be organized.[12]

Again, we should distinguish here between different coordination mechanisms. Phillips (1966) has postulated that the various interfirm linkages differ in terms of the number of firms that they are able to fully connect. Different types of networks thus have different size limits. In particular, other conditions being equal, it may be hypothesized that only formal and centralized organizational links such as associations of firms and cartels will be able to coordinate a large number of firms (Pfeffer and Salancik 1978: 179).

There is little research on this variable. Pfeffer and Salancik cite a survey by Stigler (1974) on sixty trade associations in which some indicators of the importance of the associative mechanism in the industry (such as the size of the budget and of the association's staff) were negatively correlated to degree of industry concentration. This result is consistent with the hypothesis that less formal links without central complex structures are feasible in highly concentrated industries. Stigler, however, proposes a different theoretical justification for his results which relates the number-of-firms variable to the conflict-of-interest variable. The higher the number of firms that are to be coordinated, the higher will be not only the communication and administrative costs but also the costs of opportunistic behaviors and conflict resolution procedures. Indeed, the more parties there are to an agreement in which all the parties pay a given contribution to secure a common benefit, the more incentive there will be for each individual party not to contribute its own share, if it is expected that the contributions paid by the other parties will be sufficient to obtain the common benefit. This phenomenon is known as the free-rider problem, and it is useful in demonstrating and stressing, again, that the comparative superiority of organizational forms does not depend only on the level of uncertainty and costs of information

Figure 3-2. Relative Weight of Different Interfirm Coordination Structures as a Function of the Industry Concentration Rate.

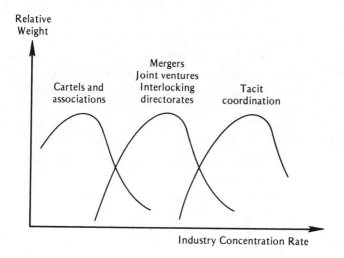

but also on the type of conflict among interests—namely, the structure of the game. Figure 3-2 shows the predicted dominant forms of organization in an industry as a function of industry rate of concentration.[13]

RD AND OTHER THEORIES: EXTERNAL CONTROL, POWER, AND EFFICIENCY

Pfeffer and Salancik (1978) and Pfeffer (1982) have presented their theory as an approach to understanding the external control of organizations. This view implies that organization structure and behavior "results from the pattern of constraints, contingencies, or demands confronting the social unit" and that they "may have little to do with the values or preferences of the actors taking the action but instead reflect . . . the constraints of external elements" (Pfeffer 1982: 8). In his recent book, Pfeffer does in fact assimilate the RD perspective with natural selection theory.[14] In effect, at this level of theory of the theory, the RD proponents fall into some inconsistency. Their assimilation of their perspective with natural selection does not seem justified if one considers the scientific basis for RD as distinct from the image its proponents have sought to endow it with.

In the first place, the natural selection approach does study the kinds of organization that are capable of surviving in a given environment, regardless of the reason and objectives that led to the selection of the particular type of organization. Aldrich (1979) points out that the ecological perspective is indifferent to the sources of organizational change, which may result for many different reasons, including random changes. The environment "chooses" the type of organization in the sense that it determines organization forms' differential survival.

By contrast, the RD perspective is based on an explicit hypothesis about the preferences of the firm as a conscious, rational actor. This actor/firm prefers organizational arrangements that reduce its dependence on outside actors to other arrangements, even if those arrangements may be internally more efficient. This type of firm prefers organizational forms that increase the dependence of other actors on itself. This means pursuing asymmetrical dependence to one's own advantage, which is equivalent to the pursuit of power. Firms can pursue power in situations of imperfect competition, and in these situations they are free to choose a variety of power-oriented strategic behaviors and are loosely subject to natural selection control.

It follows that RD is *not* a theory of external control, as Pfeffer (1982) has postulated by contrasting it with theories in which the organization is seen as the outcome of rational choice (among theories of rational organizational choice he includes structural contingency theory, the organizational failure framework, and Marxist theory). RD is a model of rational choice of organizational structures, based on specific hypotheses about the firm preference structure. As Pfeffer himself states elsewhere, "Resource dependence, although arguing from the perspective of the external control of organizations, and incorporating a coalition model of organzations (Cyert and March 1963) has more elements of rational action and rational choice embedded within it than does population ecology" (1982: 205).

Second, the incorporation of a coalition model of internal organization further weakens the hypothesis of external control. Indeed, Pfeffer and Salancik (1978) deal with internal organization by reference to models, especially from Europe (Crozier 1963; Hickson et al. 1971), that further developed the Cyert and March notion that internal organization is the outcome of negotiation between internal actors (individuals, groups, and organizational units) with different organizational goals (such as levels of production, inventories, sales, or profits) and with private goals of maintaining or increasing their own power. It would therefore seem inevitable that if politics within the firm is crucial to determining organizational behavior and structure, such behavior and structure cannot strictly be determined by exogenous factors. That is, organizational forms cannot be predicted merely on the basis of environmental constraints, as European authors have argued (Crozier and Friedberg 1977; Child 1972).

Still, RD arguments on the whole have put more emphasis on power pursuit than on external control. On this point there is a controversy with the M&H approach. The latter, in many respects, seems to be a rival explanation of the same phenomena.

Pfeffer (1982: 206) holds that

The market failures approach with its economics heritage, argues from an efficiency point of view. Vertical integration, the choice of structural form, and the choice of the form of the employment relationship are all presumed to be governed by efficiency concerns. There is a presumption of competitive pressure to force efficiency on organizations. The resource dependence perspective, on the other hand, argues that the principal concern motivating integration is the attempt to reduce uncertainty and that this uncertainty reduction will be pursued even at the expense of profits, albeit subject at some level to a profit constraint when mergers among business firms are considered. Concerned more with issues of power and politics both within the firm and between firms, resource dependence essentially argues . . . from the perspective of power maintenance and power acquisition.

Although accepted by many proponents of the other view (Williamson and Ouchi 1981; Teece 1981a), this argument is unsatisfactory for several reasons.

Let us take the issue of how to explain vertical integration between firms. It is one of the most highly debated points and one of the few on which empirical evidence is available. M&H explains vertical integration in terms of the parties to a vertical transaction being locked into the transaction (that is, being reciprocally irreplaceable) under conditions of uncertainty provided that the transaction is a recurring one. RD predicts that vertical integration will occur in line with interfirm transactional interdependences that are most intense (in terms of transaction volume) and most critical (in terms of irreplaceability and uncertainty controlled by the other party). Rephrased this way, these explanations are more similar to each other than their respective proponents might suggest. Both predict vertical growth in firms not in the direction of profit maximizing acquisitions but in the direction of existing interfirms links where these are problematic. The reasons given for a relation's becoming problematic are also similar: (1) the lack of alternatives or the irreplaceable nature of resources supplied (that is, specificity of investments); (2) the importance of transaction in terms of recurrence or volume; and (3) a state of uncertainty, in the absence of which, as both perspectives stress, interdependence between small numbers of firms can be resolved by assisted (mixed) forms of market contracting. Then, the criticism raised by some authors in the OFF school (Williamson and Ouchi 1981; Teece 1981a) about theories that explain the growth of firms in terms of power (if the objective were power, growth would be endemic and not selective in just some directions and in just some industries, as experience shows) does not apply in the case of RD.

The theoretic reasons that RD and M&H propose the advantages of hierarchies over markets do not differ much either because both perspectives stress the possibility of conflicts being resolved by authority based on unified property rights.

On the diversification issue the predictions from the two perspectives are also consistent, particularly the OFF hypothesis that a diversified and divisionalized firm will more closely approximate the profit maximization hypothesis than will a firm with a functional structure, in which integration strategies often prevail. Indeed, looking at the findings of Pfeffer and Salancik on mergers from a slightly different angle, we can infer that profit maximization predicts corporate growth by diversification more accurately than it predicts growth by integration. In fact, analyzing the profitability of a large number of acquired firms throughout the 1950s and 1960s, Pfeffer and Salancik (1978: 134) found that "firms acquired for horizontal expansion or vertical integration were less profitable than firms acquired for diversification."

Both perspectives construe organization principally as a function of the firm's overall goals, centered on reducing the costs of transactional interdependence. But both perspectives include expanded models in which the particular objectives of the internal actors are important. Both these cases assume that such objectives are aimed basically at increasing the resources controlled by subunits or subteams in the firm. We are referring for M&H to Williamson's (1964, 1970) economics of discretional behavior and for RD to Pfeffer and Salancik's (1974a, 1974b) research on power-oriented appropriations in budgetary processes. In the discretionary behavior mode, there are objectives of controlling resources, or power, that lead to corporate growth's being more marked and less selective. Within RD, the research on budgetary decisionmaking carried out by Pfeffer and Salancik actually corroborates Williamson's discretionary behavior model. This research investigated the processes whereby resources are allocated among the units of an organizational system in order to discover to what degree they were determined by principles of system global efficiency or by the power goals of the units. The organization studied, a university, was certainly of a special type because power objectives could be expected to be of major importance. It would be possible and, indeed, desirable to repeat the same kind of research on corporate organizations. In the case of the university, an efficiency criterion was identified for internal resource allocation. This was represented both by the level of demand from students for certain types of course and by the teaching load of the corresponding faculty.[15] The determinants for allocating funds among the various departments were both teaching loads and relative power of the departments. Among power indicators, the best predictors of departmental allocations were the relative importance (or percentage of representatives) of the department on budget committees and its average percentage representation on all the committees.

This type of research, applied to business organizations, could be interesting. It might show the degree to which the allocation of resources (both financial and human) is determined by criteria of overall efficiency, such as profitability, as opposed to criteria of subunits power (these power criteria being irrespective of the criticality of such units for firm profitability). For example, in the case of Williamson's M-form hypothesis, one could assess whether power indicators of first-level units are better predictors of resource allocation in functional structures than in divisional structures. Indeed, such a test of the M-form hypothesis, based on research on the decisionmaking processes, would be much stronger than the simple correlation between firm structure and overall long-term profitability, as is found in existing research.

In summary, aside from differences of language and style, the M&H and RD perspectives have relevant areas of substantial overlap, some differences in the respective fields of application, and few truly contrasting predictions—among the latter, it is worth stressing that RD, as currently formulated, does not predict any case of return from a hierarchical form to a market form. In effect, a development of research from the resource dependence perspective on disintegration phenomena does in fact appear to be stymied until *power* objectives are translated into *resource accumulation* objectives. A preference for the possession of resources will lead to a preference for the firm's growth. Even so, this hypothesis is by no means necessary. Moreover, it contrasts with the acknowledgment that the basic source of power is not in itself the possession of resources but, in more general terms, asymmetric dependence. It is in fact just as reasonable to assume that, in many cases, the presence of internal actors' power objectives will raise obstacles to the firm's growth. This would be the case, for instance, where preferential access to external information cannot be maintained by a particular subunit if the source of uncertainty is internalized to the advantage of the whole firm—that is, by reducing its overall dependence on external factors. For example, a marketing department's interest in maintaining contacts with a few important customers on which the firm depends but that are inaccessible to other internal actors would conflict with the firm's overall interest in internalizing or otherwise tightly controlling such links. Again, any decision to spin off parts of the firm into separate units may be explained as a decision to reduce interdependence between internal actors—that is, as a result of a power game between internal actors. For example, a popular explanation in Italy for the recent widespread phenomenon of disintegration of production in mechanical, textile, and other industries is that management's power objectives have been to reduce its dependence on trade unions. Although this seems superficial for various cases, it is true that in many other cases this power objective has actually played a role as a motive for boundaries reduction. For the time being, both the OFF and RD perspectives have very much overlooked these effects of power motives on boundary reduction.

NOTES

1. In Williamson's analytic model a composite utility function of the following form is maximized:

$$\text{Max} \quad U = U\,(S, M, \pi - \pi_o - T)$$

subject to $\pi \geqslant \pi_o + T$, where S and M are staff and slack expenses and appear, in the developed expression, both among costs and among revenues. $\pi - \pi_o - T$ is discretionary profit after taxes.

2. See note 1. The utility function of the ith manager will be of the type

$$U_i = U_i\,(S, M, \pi - \pi_o - T)$$

where S represents staff expenses, M represents slack, and $\pi - \pi_o - T$ discretionary profits. In general, for m different objectives Y_j the function will be $U_i = U_i\,(Y_1, \ldots, Y_j, \ldots, Y_m)$.

3. In effect, for these authors, as for most of the other proponents of systemic organization theory, the notion of the organizational boundary is different from that of the boundary of the firm as defined by property rights and contracts, whereas the two concepts are unified in the OFF perspective. There is therefore a problem of terminology with respect to the OFF perspective. According to OFF, changing the boundaries means changing the coverage of rights of ownership and hierarchical control. In RD theory this is just one particular case of change in an organizational boundary, which is located "where the discretion of the organization to control an activity is less than the discretion of another organization or individual to control that activity" (Pfeffer and Salancik 1978: 32). Organizational boundaries, defined in these wider terms, can thus also be

changed by organizational means of exercising influence other than hierarchical control.

4. These findings cover 854 mergers between firms in all sectors of manufacturing industry and oil production and refining. The correlation and regression analysis was also effected by taking a measurement of the percentage of *value* of the assets acquired in industry *j* by firms in industry *i*, showing a similar but weaker correlation.

5. Pfeffer and Salancik then also controlled that other variables, expressing possible objectives such as profitability and industry concentration, were less predictive of the direction of mergers than the transactional interdependence variable.

6. An interesting finding is that the correlation between horizontal integration in a particular industry and profitability in that industry, even though weak, is negative. This tendency of less profitable industries to merge is the opposite of what would be predicted on the basis of economic theory (Pfeffer and Salancik 1978: 124).

7. Transactional interdependence between industries explains 49.2 percent of the variance in M_{ij}. Competitive and transactional interdependence within an industry together explain 37.8 percent of the variance in M_{ii}.

8. Although profitability plays a greater role in diversification choices, it is possible—and necessary—to give an explanation of why a diversified firm should be more efficient than market in allocating resources according to profitability. This explanation has been given by recent M&H contributions, in terms of high transaction costs in the transfers of know-how and in the capital market (Teece, 1980, 1982). On this issue, see the Conclusions in Chapter 7.

9. The formation of social norms of behavior between firms has also been investigated with attention to how the collectivity of firms protects their general common interests. The various forms of managerial socialization have been studied mainly in Marxist-inspired research that has appeared in the organization field in the United States and that has aimed at empirically testing the foundations and relevance of the concept of class. Pfeffer (1981) describes various examples, such as existing empirical evidence that firms coordinate their political (such as voting) behavior much more than their economic behavior (Whitt 1980) and that social norms aimed at protecting and promoting common perception of interests are created by common membership to social, friendship, and family circles (Moore 1979).

10. *Interlocking directorates* are defined as the presence on one board of directors of members of other boards of directors (or firms' supervisory boards in general). Here, again, the RD school claims that these reduce uncertainty and mutual dependence and rejects the traditional explanation

that they increase availability of management skills or act as a control syndicate.

11. As in the discussion of mergers, the authors note that their findings contradict in part the traditional economic explanations of joint ventures that claim that mergers share risk and gather resources. These hypotheses suggest that joint ventures occur most frequently in industries where there is little concentration.

12. In terms of empirical research, the authors propose the following regression formula for both joint ventures and interlocking directorates:

$$Y_i = aX_1 X_2$$

where Y_i is the number of linkages between firms; X_1 the rate of concentration in the industry (a variable representing the number of firms to be coordinated), and X_2 the absolute value of the difference between the industry rate of concentration and the average value in all industries (a variable representing the degree of competitive uncertainty in that industry, according to the U-shaped relation hypothesis with the level of concentration).

13. The yardsticks that can be employed to measure the weight of the different types of linkages, as commonly used in the research mentioned in this paragraph, are the number of interfirm communications realized through each type of mechanism, indicators of the value of the assets involved, or indicators of the organizational size of the coordinating structure. The variable of the industry rate of concentration compounds the effects of at least two of the variables that influence the comparative advantages of coordination options—that is, competitive uncertainty and the number of firms to be linked.

14. The natural selection or population ecology theory of organizations is discussed in Chapter 5.

15. This parameter, the number of teaching units, was constructed as the product of the number of students and the number of hours in each course. As a yardstick of faculty power a principal nonobtrusive measure was taken that was the proportional representation in the main committees with decisionmaking power over the allocation of resources.

4 ORGANIZATIONAL LEARNING

The organization theories discussed in previous chapters provide models for understanding organization design based on given objectives. According to these models, effective organization structures may vary according to a firm's objectives or to the different preferences that exist in conflict with each other. The organization research described thus far explains efficient organization structures in terms of cause-and-effect relationships, given certain assumptions as to the structure of preferences.

There are two limitations to this kind of approach. First, as with any cause-and-effect model, some variances in organization structures cannot be explained within the model because of factors that have not been taken into account by the model. From the standpoint of rational design, these factors represent friction vis-à-vis the model. For instance, a rational decision to acquire a firm linked by critical interdependence or to allocate a dominant proportion of resources to an organizational subunit faced with critical uncertainties may be distorted by perception errors about where the critical factors are located.

Second, various aspects of the organization may not be chosen on the basis of objectives but may be tried without clear preferences being defined in advance. Where the consequences of an organizational choice are unclear in terms of both efficiency and the power of the parties concerned, the formation of the organization can pro-

81

ceed only on a trial-and-error basis, by testing one solution and assessing it in retrospect (Simon 1957; March and Simon 1958; Cyert and March 1963; Winter 1975). The process of organizing starts with undefined preferences, and objectives are eventually learned a posteriori by observing effects (March 1978). The literature on adaptive reasoning, represented by the authors cited above, has tended to concentrate not on organizational choice but on corporate learning processes applied to economic behavior (such as external decisions involving pricing and investment).

To find examples of organizational choice that justify the adaptive (reasonable if not rational) approach, one has to think of those aspects of organizations having consequences that cannot be assessed in advance against major objectives. Organizational choices of this kind, for example, involve the choice and placement of individuals within the organization. Indeed, it is notoriously difficult to predict the potential performance of any particular individual because in many cases, different individuals will appear, in advance, to be largely interchangeable. It is no coincidence that organizational learning models have been applied mostly to organization issues such as career processes, performance evaluation, group formation, and interpersonal dynamics—that is, how to match individuals with roles and with other individuals (see research described below in the section on random career processes). This indeterministic approach centers on phenomena that lie largely outside the scope of the other theories covered thus far in this book.

The discussion of this approach in this chapter first presents ideas about the perception and subjective reconstruction of the environment through the eyes of each individual or group of individuals belonging to an organization. It then proceeds to the specific models of adaptive organizational behavior advanced by the indeterministic school. In approaching the indeterminists in this way a caveat is needed. The main proponents of an indeterministic approach (Weick 1979a, 1979b; Cohen, March, and Olsen 1972, 1976; March 1978; Staw 1980; Hedberg, Nystrom, and Starbuck 1976) tend to advance their ideas as a general theory of organization. Here, however, they are considered as a special case of organization theories. They focus on a fundamentally different domain—that is, on particular processes that may vary in importance in different types of organization and under different circumstances. The universalistic emphasis of some indeterministic authors has in fact been criticized, but it has played a thought-provoking role against the efficiency-oriented rationalism that pervades the U.S. ethos. In any case, this chapter reviews the assumptions and research results of this orientation in the positive science terms of how the considered variables affect organizational structures but does not follow the main contributors into their broad generalizations.

BASIC ASSUMPTIONS: THE ENACTED ENVIRONMENT

Those who take the indeterminist perspective have criticized the deterministic concept of the relationships between an organization and its environment that prevails in the systemic theory of organization. In contrast to the notion of an objective external environment to which an organization has to adapt itself, the indeterminists postulate the concept of the enacted environment (Weick 1979a) that the organization itself selects and creates. The environment is not, nor can it be, conceived as an independent variable that conditions the organization, unless one overlooks important mediating and feedback effects. The indeterministic perspective stresses two components of enactment processes: (1) knowledge processes that are mediated by perception and lead to fallible cognitive models of reality and (2) interaction processes between the behaviors of internal and external actors—that is, changes in the environment to which the firm chooses to respond that may be induced by its own responses.

Knowledge

Although the importance of perception has been long recognized, it has received more attention in studies on individual behavior than in those on organizations. Perception of any event implies the decoding and interpretation of messages that are feasible only through the mental schemas of the subject (Simon 1957; Neisser 1976; Axelrod 1973, 1976). It has been extensively demonstrated that individuals tend to persist in their schemas, bodies of concepts and beliefs, and theories of cause-and-effect relationships without looking for or even being able to perceive information that can invalidate these beliefs (Einhorn and Hogarth 1978; Tversky and Kahneman 1982; Einhorn 1982; Ross and Anderson 1982). Similar phenomena have been investigated at the organizational level by March and Simon (1958). More recently, the indeterminists have focused on the process of perception and cognition in organizations, largely taking their lead from Simon's thought. Their approach to the organization is based on cognitive analysis, centered on how information is handled (Weick 1979b). They do not focus on emotional and affective dynamics but have sought to model different forms of rationality, or at least of thought. These are very weak or bounded forms of rationality, indeed. They include retrospective rationality and the deliberate use of randomness or foolishness that can reasonably or sensibly (March 1978) lead men to action when information ambiguity blocks traditional means/end prospective rationality.

From this perspective, the firm must select from an environment that is seen as a mass of redundant information (Simon 1977). The first major subjective mediation in constructing one's own environment is thus to allocate attention to it. As proposed by March and Simon (1958), the issues and information that an organization deals with are the outcome of (1) the causal structure of the environment, (2) the causal map the organization has elaborated of the environment, (3) the chronological order in which the information and issues appear, and (4) chance.

Second, the environment is constructed not only because it is selectively perceived but also because information must be given a meaning. The meaning will depend on the mental schemes, models, or theories of the subject. In the case of a collective subject such as a firm, the indeterministic school has made considerable use of the paradigm concept proposed by Kuhn (1962) in his analysis of how scientific communities operate. When applied to a firm, an organizational paradigm represents all the knowledge and theories shared and used by organization members (Argyris and Schön 1978). Some authors have studied the processes of communication and integration of cognitions that lead to the formation of collective organizational knowledge (Duncan and Weiss 1979).

The central idea of a research perspective on organizational knowledge has been formulated by Karl Weick (1979b), who has advanced the intriguing concept of the firm as a scientific community with self-interest. This line of thinking, however, has not been developed very far. Indeed, the emphasis has been on the analysis of the objects that represent organizational paradigms—that is, beliefs, cognitive maps, schemas, and myths rather than on the laws that regulate the change and self-correction of these objects.

The analysis of the development of knowledge and values has been largely in terms of their tendency for remaining somewhat constant. Inertia and confirmation biases have been the prevalent focus in the two base disciplines—cognitive psychology and sociology of knowledge—concerned with analyzing the individual's deviations from rational learning behavior patterns in the direction of self-protection (Einhorn 1982). The sociology of scientific communities, as advanced by Kuhn's school, has highlighted, in an antipositivistic posture, how scientific paradigms tend to reproduce themselves, changing only under extreme conditions in which they are disrupted by external events or when they fail to provide an explanation for a mounting number of phenomena that exceeds scientists' tolerance for incoherence (Kuhn 1962).

This emphasis on the inertia of knowledge—which becomes magnified when incorporated into plans for action and organizational procedures—has led the indeterminists to prescribe a solution in the form of organizational behaviors that rediscover the innovation potential of play, chance, and trial and error (Cohen, March, and Olsen 1976). Weick (1979a: 86) describes the prevailing content of managers' overly rigid mental habits about causal relations:

> Most managers get into trouble because they forget to think in circles. I mean this literally. Managerial problems persist because managers continue to believe that there are such things as unilateral causation, independent and dependent variables, origins, and terminations. Examples are everywhere: leadership style affects productivity, parents socialize children, stimuli affect responses, ends affect means, desires affect actions. Those assertions are wrong because each of them demonstrably also operates in the opposite direction: productivity affects leadership style (Lowin and Craig 1968), children socialize parents (Osofsky 1971), responses affect stimuli (Gombrich 1960), means affect ends (Hirschman and Lindblom 1962), actions affect desires (Bem 1967). In every one of these examples causation is circular, not linear. And the same thing holds true for most organizational events.

Some proposed prescriptions to solve this problem are to replace deductive causal thinking by thinking in circles by association of concepts (Weick 1979a), and to conduct social experiments. March points out that a fundamental source of innovation lies in the ability to experiment through trial and error, involving action that is difficult to justify *a priori*. The ability to behave this way is a desirable management skill, and one of the tasks of organization theory is to devise a technology or a normative theory of action antecedent to thought (March 1978: 79).

Interaction

The prescriptive aspect of the indeterministic approach does not extend, perhaps purposely, much beyond this kind of advice. It is relatively undeveloped. On the other hand, the descriptive dimension is well developed and covers many areas, including the role of ambiguity and the social construction of reality.

A fundamental step in this direction was the modification of the concept of environment from perceived environment to enacted environment (Weick 1979a). *Enactment* does not refer merely to the ability to act on, or change, the environment. Unlike the concepts of altered and negotiated environments postulated in the resource-dependence perspective, the enacted environment does not imply a conscious change made in the environment according to the firm's objectives. Rather, the environment is modified by the presence of a firm because of the unforeseen effects and the undesired, nonpursued consequences arising from action taken by the firm. In other words, the focus is on uncontrolled change, of which there are at least two types: (1) self-fulfilling prophecies and (2) the magnifying effect of small variations (or minor actions) (Weick 1979a).

Self-fulfilling prophecies are exemplified, for instance, in the experimental study by Kelley and Stahelski (1970) and cited by Weick (1979: 162) of prophecies that players in competitive games make regarding the behavior of other players. The experiment was carried out using the Prisoner's Dilemma game and shows how the presence of some players who do not trust the others (in the sense that they expect their adversaries not to cooperate) does in fact lead to the adversaries' taking a conflicting stance, even in cases where they would have preferred to cooperate.

To illustrate the amplification of the small-variations phenomenon one can consider the voluntary formation of social and professional groups either in firms, in public organizations, or in society. The resulting organization structure, which in this case may be the formation of a peer group, will in many cases be hard to explain as the effect of one or more environmental causes or as a rational means of achieving given objectives.

A case in point is the formation of a strong and highly qualified group of organizational behavior academicians in Sweden. A traditional explanation, based on cause-and-effect relationships, would be that Sweden is a socially oriented country with an affluent economy and strong trade unions. Another explanation, based on the assumption of rational behavior aimed at achieving objectives, would be that the Minister of Education had decided to develop certain disciplines on the basis of some kind of collective cost/benefit analysis. Still another rational means/ends explanation would see the rise of the group as a result of effective resource accumulation strategies by a nascent disciplinary group in the interests of increasing its own power.

Yet the explanation of why the group was formed may also be attributed to interaction. Someone, somewhere, for some reason, starts to get involved in organizational behavior. In order to keep the work going, he or she must seek co-workers. Others may move into the field as imitators. The existing human resources create some teaching output; the existence of courses creates an audience; the audience and the course create academic positions; and so forth.

Another example described by Weick (1979a: 81) is the formation of a city in an agricultural area:

> Once the farmer opens a farm at a chance spot on it, other farmers follow his example; soon one of the farmers opens a tool shop where the farmers congregate. Later a food stand opens next to the tool shop, and a village grows. The village makes it easier to market crops, which attracts still more farmers; eventually a city develops. Now, if an analyst looks for a geographical cause as to why this particular spot and not some other became a city, he won't find it. He won't find it because "it" is not there. The amplifying processes generated the complexity. And because the final outcome is so complex, there are that many more false leads concerning "things" or single variables that could have "caused" this city to form in this place. All of these clues are misleading because none of them "caused" the city to be located in just that spot. The truth will be lost to the analyst, especially to the person who views reality as consisting solely of things and structures rather than relations and processes.

RESEARCH APPLICATIONS: RANDOM
ORGANIZATIONAL PROCESSES

The Garbage Can Model of Organizational Choice

The most important model of organizational behavior under ambiguity is the garbage can model proposed by Cohen, March, and Olsen (1972). Ambiguity is seen as the state of knowledge that characterizes the relationship between the actor and a volatile, interactive, poorly understood environment. Not only is it assumed that cause-and-effect relationships (the technologies used to produce organizational action) are unclear but also that the actors' objectives are unclear (in that members of the organization must first take action in order, possibly, to discover them). Further, even the participants in the organization are not clearly defined. In the authors' words (Cohen, March, and Olsen 1972: 1) "the boundaries of the organization are uncertain and changing; the audiences and decision makers for any particular kind of choice change capriciously." Thus, the model of organizational structures proposed considers the continuum from a normal state of uncertainty (to which a hierarchical form of organization is well suited) to a state of ambiguity (in which only loosely coupled forms of organization can survive).

In normal uncertainty conditions, the organization structure is the conventional hierarchical goal-oriented system, coordinated from a center and usually differentiated into specialized role subsystems. Whenever the organization members and their objectives are defined, and it is known how (with what techniques) acceptable solutions to the problems posed by firm's activities can be reached, these activities may be arranged in a specialized hierarchical structure. If, however, ambiguity conditions prevail, there is no longer any criteria for differentiating the structure either vertically (hierarchy of objectives) or horizontally (specialization by technique or by objectives).

To characterize such a broad sweep of organization types, Cohen, March, and Olsen adopt a special way of defining and measuring them. An organizational form can be represented by one particular combination of four sets of factors: participants in the organization, the solutions they propose, the problems they have access to, and the type of choice opportunities to which members, problems, and solutions have access. Choice opportunities are situations in which a

choice has to be made, such as contract due dates, the need to reallo-
cate financial and human resources and responsibilities, and, in general, "occasions when an organization is expected to produce behavior that can be called a decision."

A hierarchical or specialist organization represents a particular,
fixed distribution of types of choice among types of decisionmakers.
In a hierarchy, it should be possible to classify decisionmakers and
choices in order of importance, and the organization can be represented as an ensemble of permitted or forbidden arrangements between the decisionmakers and the decisions they make. For instance,
the more important decisionmakers are allotted more numerous and
more important choices. A hierarchical organization can thus be rep
resented by a decisionmakers/choice opportunity matrix of the kind
illustrated as type 1 in Table 4-1. A specialized organization will
look like type 2, in which only one type of choice is associated with
each decisionmaker. If, by contrast, it is assumed that the knowledge
needed for rational differentiation of the organization is not available, this will produce a nonsegmented structure of the kind represented in the matrix shown as type 3, in which all the decisionmakers
may take part in all types of choices. These participant/choices
matrices are called decisionmaking structures and define a type of
organizational structure.

The behavior of these structures will then depend on what types
of solution have access to each choice opportunity. In other words,
the kind of decisionmaking process characteristic of any given organization can also be represented by matrices describing the permitted
combinations between choice opportunities and the type of problems that can be dealt with when those opportunities arise, and what
type of solutions can be considered for those problems in those occasions. These problem/choice opportunities matrices are defined as
access structures, and their basic possible configurations are similar
to that of the decisionmaking structures shown in Table 4-1. An
access structure may be such that choice opportunities are distinguished by importance or by functional area, and the only solutions
that can be considered in each occasion are those belonging to the
same importance level or functional specialization, in which case the
access structure will be specialist and hierarchical. Alternatively, if
these combinations cannot be specified in a stable way because of
the lack of clear objectives or technologies, the access structure will
be unsegmented.

Table 4-1. Matrices Representing Organizational Forms as Decisionmaking Structures.

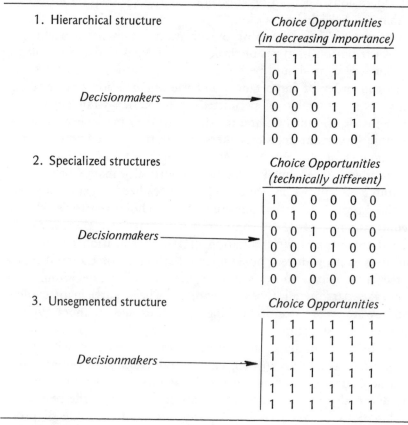

1. Hierarchical structure

Choice Opportunities
(in decreasing importance)

1	1	1	1	1	1
0	1	1	1	1	1
0	0	1	1	1	1
0	0	0	1	1	1
0	0	0	0	1	1
0	0	0	0	0	1

Decisionmakers ———→

2. Specialized structures

Choice Opportunities
(technically different)

1	0	0	0	0	0
0	1	0	0	0	0
0	0	1	0	0	0
0	0	0	1	0	0
0	0	0	0	1	0
0	0	0	0	0	1

Decisionmakers ———→

3. Unsegmented structure

Choice Opportunities

1	1	1	1	1	1
1	1	1	1	1	1
1	1	1	1	1	1
1	1	1	1	1	1
1	1	1	1	1	1
1	1	1	1	1	1

Decisionmakers ———→

Source: Cohen, March, and Olsen (1976).

Unsegmented structures behavior is context-dependent and quasi-random from a means/end point of view, as March and Shapiro (1982: 103) explain:

The specific collection of decision makers, problems and solutions that comes to be associated with a particular choice opportunity is orderly—but the logic of the ordering is temporal and contextual rather than hierarchical or consequential. At the limit, almost any solution can be associated with almost any problem—provided they are contemporaries.

In order to depict organizational behavior in this way, problems, solutions, and choices have to be considered, in principle, as independent events. Solutions are ideas, products of the participants in an organization who will produce decisions if and when they encounter problems to which such solutions can be applied and if and when opportunities arise for a choice to be made. As Cohen, March, and Olsen (1972: 1) provocatively state, under ambiguity "organizations can be viewed for some purposes as collections of choices looking for problems, issues and feelings looking for decision situations in which they might be aired, solutions looking for issues to which they might be an answer, and decision makers looking for work."

It should be noted, however, that this is a contingency. When access structures reflect knowledge of cause-and-effect relationships and the preferences of the members of the organization, they regulate in a logical fashion the links between these series of events participants, choice opportunities, problems, and solutions. Only when technologies or participants' preferences are unclear and ambiguity is present will access structures indicate that all the combinations between the four streams of events are allowed.

The type of organization characterized by unsegmented decision-making and access structures (that is, by matrices in which all combinations are permitted) has been called organized anarchy by Cohen, March, and Olsen. These authors set out to identify the variables, in this type of organization, that can affect the matches between problems, solutions, choices, and participants (that is, the organization's actions), given that these matches are not restricted by the decision-making and access structures. They thus came to delineate two further dimensions of an organizational structure that indicate the level of stress or, in the authors' words, the load on the system: the total net load on the organizational system and its internal energy distribution, defined as follows:

1. An organization has a limited total amount of energy (operationalizable, for example, as time available to each of its members) to use in solving problems.

2. This energy can be used with varying degrees of efficiency. At any given time, the organization may be characterized by a fixed coefficient of reduction in total energy, expressed by the average amount of energy wasted through inefficiency.

3. A minimum given amount of energy is needed to solve all the problems that are encountered in a given period. The closer this

minimum is to the total amount of energy available, the higher will be the total net load on the system.

4. The total available energy may be distributed in various different ways among the members of the organization. The authors concentrate on three typical distribution patterns:

- Equal distribution, where each member of the organization has the same amount of energy to devote to problemsolving;

- Unequal distribution, where the more important members have more energy available; and

- Unequal distribution, where more energy is available among the rank-and-file.

This forms the basic outline of the garbage can model. It has been tested by simulating on computer a range of organizational systems corresponding to various possible combinations of the values of the four variables characterizing an organization—that is, decisionmaking structure, access structure, system net load, and energy distribution. A further variable that influences combinations of the four elements of the organizational system (problems, solutions, choice opportunities, and participants in the organization) is the arrival time (origin or entry) of these elements into the system. In the computer simulations, a number of random sequences of the arrival time of problems and choice opportunities were used.

In looking at the results produced by these simulations, a crucial point is the general tendency displayed by the decisions reached in unsegmented structures to be closely dependent on the system net load—that is, on the amount of excess energy present in the organization. This result is consistent with the theoretical view of the role of slack resources in decisionmaking. In effect, system load is a variable that expresses the degree of organizational slack in the system, which can be defined as "the difference between the resources of the organization and the combination of demands made on it" (Cohen, March, and Olsen 1972: 12). Accordingly, the model simulations show that an increase in system load, representing a reduction in slack in terms of excess energy available to the decisionmakers, increases the number of unsolved problems and, when decisions are reached, that they tend to be simply dependent on the arrival times of the elements and on the inequalities in the slack energy available among the different participants.

The results of these simulations also provide more detailed information on the effect of changes in system load on a variety of other dimensions in the decisionmaking process. The authors have in fact calculated a set of statistics that describe these dimensions, including decisionmaking style,[1] problem latency,[2] the decisionmaker's mobility,[3] and decision difficulty.[4] They have thus been able to state (Cohen, March, and Olsen 1976: 34) that

> an increase in the net energy load on the system generally increases problem activity, decision maker activity, decision difficulty, and the uses of flight and oversight [decision styles]. Problems are less likely to be solved, decision makers are likely to shift from one problem to another more frequently, choices are likely to take longer to make and to be less likely to resolve problems.

A fundamental issue arising from these findings that is stressed by the authors is the role of chance in the behavior of any organization and the strategic effect of time that goes with it. Although these factors may affect the behavior of hierarchical and specialist organizations to some degree, they become crucial in soft systems (otherwise called loosely coupled systems) where organization becomes an invertebrate process rather than a structure. The authors assume that the behavior of pure unsegmented structures can be predicted only in accordance with the timing of events and the relative scarcity of energy. They hold that organizations very similar to this model exist, and their main example is the university. The book *Ambiguity and Choice in Organizations* (1976) contains a number of case studies on decisionmaking processes in universities, such as the election of a dean, internal reorganization processes, and the creation of new campuses, interpreted according to the garbage can model.

The empirical basis for the garbage can model is still somewhat weak. Pfeffer (1982) notes that a weak methodological point of this research lies in the way in which Cohen, March, and Olsen test their theory. They seek examples of theory, for which there may always be alternative explanations or theories that equally well explain the events observed. The alternative possibilities are rarely considered in these case studies.

In terms of its theoretical contribution, the garbage can model broadens the range of the known types of organization structure. A system in which everybody can do everything and in which the links between the various parts do not necessarily have to follow given interdependence relationships but are virtually interchangeable and separable is a concept that organization theory had previously treated primarily in terms of peer groups. Indeterminists coined the expression *loosely coupled systems* to define complex organizations that have this feature (Weick 1976, and 1979a; Cohen, March, and Olsen 1976).

The garbage can model extends the continuum of organization systems because it constructs specific models of a new type of system—the organized anarchy or loosely coupled system. This model cannot therefore be reduced to a simple emphasis on the role of chance, as has sometimes been the case. In fact, the type of environmental uncertainty and the corresponding efficient organization structures described in traditional organization theory[5] is limited (1) as to the uncertainty variable, to variability in knowledge about cause-and-effect relationships and (2) as to the dependent organizational variables, to the continuum going from mechanistic systems to highly differentiated and integrated systems to completely organic systems. Task may be unclear (Lawrence and Lorsch 1967) or unpredictable (Galbraith 1973), or the environment may be variable rather than stable (Burns and Stalker 1961). Only Thompson (1967) noted that uncertainty has at least one other important dimension in addition to clarity in cause-and-effect relationships—namely, clarity in preferences. However, he did not elaborate on the organizational consequences of this early insight. The next step is to specify how an organization can operate with ambiguous environments and preferences, and the behavioral model for such an organization was provided by the indeterministic school.

Random Career Processes

In addition to enabling models to be made of entire organizations, the indeterministic approach suggests new lines of research into specific organizational processes. In fact, various quasi-random processes can take place within organizational subsystems when the functions and processes are differentiated both vertically and horizontally. The most interesting applications of the indeterministic approach to business organizations, in which hierarchical and specialist structures tend to be the norm, thus seem to lie in studying such subprocesses rather than the entire system.

For instance, March and March (1977) studied the managerial careers subsystem. Although their particular case study covers an area of the public services (superintendents' positions in the Wisconsin school system), their methodology is of general interest for the study of career processes. The career model they construct is based on a simple, stationary Markov process. It is assumed that promotions and the length of careers can be represented as stochastic phenomena or random fluctuations regardless of the characteristics of the people concerned and the positions they hold. The model assumes that where there is a given group of people (superintendents) and a given group of jobs (superintendents' positions in education districts), the career process is defined by the probability of transition among three possible states: An individual may (1) be working as a superintendent, (2) be eligible to be a superintendent or (3) leave the process and become ineligible. The probabilities of transition between these states are fixed and homogeneous for all the individuals and jobs—that is, they "do not depend on any property of the individual, district, pairing, or time, and each year for each superintendency is an independent trial" (March and March 1977: 387).

For example, the expected length of a superintendent's job will simply depend on a fixed parameter P, which is homogeneous throughout the system and equal to the probability that the job will continue for an additional year.[6] Parameter P, like the other parameters necessary to define the process,[7] is estimated as the historical frequency of transitions based on a period running from 1940 to 1972.[8] The resulting career process model, is based on probabilities of transition that are stationary in time and homogeneous for all individuals and positions, is shown in Figure 4-1.

The theoretical distributions predicted by the random process model are then compared with the distributions observed in all the variables characteristic of the career process involved. These are (1) the length of the superintendent's jobs, (2) the number of superintendencies recorded in each district over the period covered, (3) career length or number of superintendencies held by each individual, and (4) the degree of individual mobility between districts. In general, it was found that the deviations between theoretic and actual distributions are not wide. Thus, a simple stationary homogeneous stochastic model predicts, in a reasonably accurate way, events (in this case, promotions) that are assumed to be governed by rational performance assessment and selection procedures.

Figure 4-1. Model of a Random Career Process: Transition Probabilities between States.

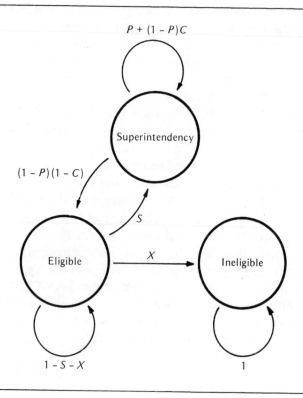

Source: March and March (1977).

However, because deliberate performance-dependent career procedures are actually applied in the Wisconsin school system, as in all other organizations, the observed quasi-random nature of management careers calls for some explanation. The authors postulate that apparent randomness may be partly due to a quasi-indistinguishability between one manager and another, as a result of socializing and training received before taking on managerial jobs. Another part of random fluctuations in actual promotions is hypothesized to be due to errors in observing and assessing performance. Thus, "within the population of superintendents, success is almost random, as it is within any control process, if the process is effective enough, or the observation tools poor enough, to make the variance in performance only a little greater than the error variance of the procedures by which it is observed" (March and March 1977: 406).

Despite these general results, the authors found a number of significant discrepancies between the actual distribution of career events and their theoretical random distributions. First, the process is not homogeneous in all respects, in that the probabilities of transition depend on certain features of the districts; for example, in larger districts superintendents' jobs last longer. Even so, these deviations from the random pattern derive more from the characters of positions (the types of districts) than from those of the individuals and the roles concerned. More significant, because they are linked to variations between individuals, are instances in which the process is not stationary—that is, where there are variations in the transition probabilities over time. For example, the longer a superintendency has lasted, the longer will be its expected additional duration, and the number of superintendencies already held by an individual increases his or her chances of being given another such job. This leads the authors to hypothesize that, if not rational selection procedures, there are at least reciprocal learning and adaptation phenomena between people and roles. Referring back to March and Simon's (1958) early insights, they write: "bilateral specialization of organization and employee is a likely consequence of their association over time," thus "after some time in a match, each of the two partners could leave the match only at prohibitive cost" (March and March 1977: 405). In other words, even where rational selection of individuals is not to be expected—because of ambiguity in performance evaluation—it is likely that individuals at least rationally select behavioral responses (or learn) in order to match roles or other individuals' behaviors.

ORGANIZATIONAL LEARNING AND THE LIMITS OF RANDOM PROCESSES

The previous discussion on deviations from pure random processes suggests some conclusions about the scope of random models of organizational behavior. Random organizational choices—encounters between people and roles, people and problems, and solutions and choice opportunities that could also have been produced by chance—

are useful in situations where little information is available *a priori*. If the comparative advantages produced by different combinations of individuals and organizational roles, sellers and buyers, individuals and other individuals operating in cooperation, and so forth cannot be known *a priori*, the alternative organizational options are almost indistinguishable. There is thus a (meta-) rational basis for dealing with them as though they have the same expected value—that is, for following a random choice strategy. Indeed, though it is reasonable to devise organizational solutions at the outset in this way, it is unlikely that information about the results will be so ambiguous as to justify continuing with the random process subsequently. If they cannot be predicted *a priori*, then factors such as the quality of colleagues, the success of an individual in a job, and the results of a particular organizational choice as to how to delegate responsibilities can all be assessed *a posteriori* on the basis of experience. Thus, organizational arrangements formed or learned in ambiguous conditions will normally have a rational justification, even if this can be assessed only *a posteriori* and will be based on observing the degree of success of the attempted solutions.

Both March and March (1978) and Weick (1979b) have investigated the ways in which these learning processes occur. A main interest here, though, has been again to look at sources of biases, errors, and subjectivity that may impair this form of retrospective rationality. In their view, organizational arrangements and behaviors succeed or fail by a nondeterministic, inescapably biased process.

In seeking to understand such distortions, March and March (1978) pursued their study of the nonstationary aspects of career processes in the Wisconsin school system. They demonstrated that some of the variations observed in individual performances cannot legitimately be attributed to underlying differences in individuals' abilities. These judgments depend on variations that would come about in any case by chance, both in the failure and success outcomes' series and in performance measures. Moreover, these errors are magnified by the typical biases of human judgment under uncertainty, such as the common sampling error (Tversky and Kahneman 1971): Learning processes are commonly biased by the tendency to consider too small samples of observations for providing a sound base to the judgment we want to make (e.g., we tend to consider too short series of performance results for evaluating an individual's capacity on a job).

Actually, a number of other types of recurring shortcomings in inference and judgment in learning processes might be added to the sampling error mentioned by March and March (1978) to demonstrate that learning processes are generally prone to highly simplifying heuristic shortcuts rather than follow rational learning models. Among the wide inventory of human judgment biases provided by the behavioral decision theory (Kahneman, Slovic, and Tversky 1982; Einhorn and Hogarth 1982; Bazerman 1985), specific examples of learning process biases are insensitivity to prior probability, overconfidence, self-serving biases in causal attributions, insensitivity to negative evidence, illusory correlation, and inferential asymmetries in causal thinking.

In addition to individual learning processes, Weick (1979a) has placed greater emphasis on the cognitive structure of *organizational* learning processes under ambiguity. With perhaps some more trust in the possibilities of human thinking than James March, Weick rather than focusing only on biases developed models of learning processes as natural selection processes applied to social behavior.[9] His interest is mainly on creative processes that produce new knowledge that has not been distilled from information already available. In fact, where no information is available to allow a reasoned identification and assessment of alternatives to be made *a priori*, as in truly new problems, a learning process can be seen as starting with a blind trial (a random choice) corresponding to the phase of variation in an evolutionary process. The marvel of the evolutionary mechanism is in fact that it produces innovation and learning, although variation is unjustified (Weick 1979a: 23) or blind (Campbell 1960). Selection mechanisms based on observed successes and failures of these tried organizational behaviors will cause their differential survival. Organizational behaviors of success will tend to be spread by individuals or groups imitating each other and by the principle of reinforcement (that is, repeat actions that have been shown to succeed and abandon those that have been proven to fail). Organizational structures and mechanisms will ultimately tend to stabilize and preserve selected behaviors and thus to bring about memorized behavior.

Organizational solutions governed by this social learning process will occur as a truly natural selection process, in which entire organization systems may either survive or be eliminated if they do not fit the environment and the behaviors selected by other systems. In other words, Weick considers that a natural selection mechanism that determines the differential survival of learned organizational structures also operates on organizational systems that have been formed by adaptive, sociocultural selection processes rather than by rational design.

This review of the indeterministic approach has highlighted the subjective factors that condition, among other processes, the natural selection process as applied to organizations. As Weick (1979a) points out, the selecting environment is itself selected. Any organizational environment is enacted—that is, it is a product rather than an input of successful actions and cognitive processes. Research into the indeterministic approach is thus directed at investigating the processes of evolution rather than its results, which it considers indetermined. By contrast, the population ecology approach, examined in Chapter 5, starts with a given (or already selected) environment (say, a particular industry), ignores the influence of judgmental biases in perceiving the environment and the possibility of modifying it, and defines a model of the resulting (selected) organization forms depending on the state of the environment.

NOTES

1 . A decisionmaking style is a recurring pattern found in combining problems and solutions with choice opportunities. For example, if a problem enters a budget committee as a choice opportunity and is solved after a given time in that same committee, the style will be the familiar one of decision by problem resolution. If, however, problems coexist with one choice opportunity for some time without being solved and then shift to other opportunities where they are solved, then the style is decisionmaking by flight. A third decisionmaking style is oversight: "If a choice is activated when problems are attached to other choices and if there is energy available to make the new choice quickly, it will be made without any attention to existing problems and with a minimum of time and energy" (Cohen, March, and Olsen 1972: 8).

2. *Problem latency* is defined as the number of periods of time in which problems continue to coexist with one or more choice opportunities and provides a yardstick of how difficult it is to solve those problems.

3. The mobility of decisionmakers is defined as the number of times that decisionmakers move from one choice opportunity to another.

4. *Difficulty in decisionmaking* is defined as the number of time periods in which choice opportunities remain open and active and provides a measure of the overall difficulty of the decisionmaking process.

5. I refer to SCT and its immediate predecessor models, such as the continuum between mechanistic and organic systems as defined by Burns and Stalker (1961).

6. The model identifies a series of expressions that give the probability distributions of some main variables in the career process, such as the expected length of a job, the number of jobs held in succession by an individual, the number of individuals holding a job in succession, and so forth. For example, in the case of job length T, the probability that the job will last for t years is given by

$$P\{T = t\} = P^{t-1}(1 - P) \qquad (t = 1, 2, 3, \dots)$$

7. The other parameters are

C: the conditional probability that if a superintendency ends in a given year, the individual who held it will be found in another superintendency in the following year;

S: the probability that a former superintendent, who is still eligible in a given year, will be appointed the following year;

X: the probability that a former superintendent who is eligible in a given year is no longer eligible in the following year.

8. For instance, the probability $(1 - P)$ that a superintendency terminates in the following year is estimated as the ratio between the number of terminations of superintendencies that started between 1940 and 1972 (1,715) and the total number of job years in which such terminations were possible (10,701).

9. The main reference here is to Campbell (1960, 1970), the leading exponent of the social evolution approach.

5 THE NATURAL SELECTION OF ORGANIZATIONS

From standpoint of the individual firm as a decisionmaker, effective organization may either be designed rationally or learned adaptively. The more competitive the firm's environment, the more important will be the design or learning of fit organizational solutions. Errors or inertia that intervene to slow, distort, or stop organizational change and adaptation in a competitive environment will allow superior organizations to survive and cause inferior ones to fail.

The natural selection of organizational forms thus differs from design and learning—the two other processes of selecting organizational structures and processes. Natural selection is an external process that, in competitive conditions, acts irrespective of whether or not the decisionmakers are aware of (1) the environment in which they are operating and (2) the organizational solutions that have been or should have been adopted. However, the degree of severity of the natural selection process hinges both on the degree of competition and on the behavior of all those subjects competing for the same scarce resources. Furthermore, the natural selection model takes a given environment, or resource space as an assumption. But in a wider perspective, it should always be remembered that this environment is the result of a positioning choice and is not a factor that can never be affected by the firm. Then, the population ecology of organizations (PEO) that is discussed in this chapter can be seen as an analytic normative tool for evaluating the most efficient organizational forms in different types of competitive environments, not as a deterministic model of the evolution of organizational structures.

PEO is a relatively recent line of research, principally developed by Hannan and Freeman (1977). The empirical work is in a relatively early stage of development compared with the theoretical model. Even so, PEO research has produced interesting results. For example, it has shown that when populations of competing organizations are considered, it is not always true that in uncertain environments highly flexible organizational structures are superior to highly specialized and formalized structures, as is maintained by commonly accepted organization theory (see the section later in this chapter on competition between generalist and specialist organizational forms in a dynamic environment). The following discussion covers the main research findings of the PEO school and how they relate to propositions on the same phenomena treated in other theories discussed in this book.

BASIC ASSUMPTIONS

The conditions that most favor the actions of natural selection mechanisms on business organizations are a combination of severe interfirm competition and internal structural inertia. Hannan and Freeman (1977)—start by observing that organizational change processes within firms are not as endemic as the traditional organizational systems theory suggest and that there are several powerful forces of inertia: (1) There may be a lack of (or distortion in) information on the environment to which the firm should be adapting; (2) a tendency exists for the organization to perpetuate itself as a result of its latent functions (as Merton called them) as a generator of consensus and cultural paradigms; (3) there can be conflict of interests within the firm that increase the cost of reorganization; and (4) external conflict with other firms may reduce the probability of success of any organizational strategy because "we should not presume that a course of action that is adaptive for a single organization facing some changing environment will be adaptive for many competing organizations adopting a similar strategy" (Hannan and Freeman 1977: 932).

These forces of inertia can be generated by errors or avoidable dysfunctions. Yet they also may be insurmountable when they are due to a high degree of uncertainty or be desired when they have been developed to protect legitimate interests. Therefore it is important to study the conditions under which particular organizational arrangements may be selected by the environment, in case organizational decisionmakers are not going to change firms' structures from within.

The natural selection of organizational forms by the environment occurs by substituting unsuccessful populations of organizations, while adaptive learning of organizational forms consists of substituting unsuccessful behavioral responses (Hannan and Freeman 1977: 929). In the PEO the level of analysis is not on individual firms but rather on populations of firms.

The concept of population is described by analogy to the biological concept of species. Indeed, as in biology, the main interest lies in explaining the variety of, or differentiations between, existing organization forms. A *population of organizations* is defined as a set of firms with the same organizational form and inhabiting the same particular environment or resource space. In fact, from an ecological standpoint, the forces that determine the survival of one kind of organizational form, or specie, rather than another derive from the common dependence of several populations of organizations on the same scarce resources (or at least on combinations of different scarce resources that have zones of intersection). The PEO theory accordingly defines economic sectors and market niches as combinations of resources that can be used by populations of organizations as follows:

1. An economic sector, or industry, is defined as a resource space with n dimensions, each of which represents one type of resource, "such as money, market segments, people, energy, physical space, and physical substances and the various combinations in which they are used." For example, "for many kinds of industries, including profit and service oriented ones, the partitioning of the resource space centers on a distinction between price-sensitive and quality conscious market segments. Other possible bases for dividing the resource space include hours of operation, convenience of location, servicing agreements, and specialization of function" (Brittain and Freeman 1980: 293).

2. "Any particular combination, or set of combinations, of resource utilization that distinguishes one organizational population from another is what we call a 'niche.' An industry, then, may include a number of distinct niches, filled to varying degrees

by specific organizational populations. Each niche is a resource base that supports a population with a given form" (Brittain and Freeman 1980: 294).

In order to advance a first hypothesis on the organization/environment relation, the authors' argument starts out from the isomorphism principle that has been the foundation for traditional applications of ecology to human systems (Hawley 1950, 1968). According to Hawley, the authors state that "the diversity of organizational forms is isomorphic to the diversity of environments. In each distinguishable environmental configuration one finds, in equilibrium, only that organizational form optimally adapted to the demands of the environments" (1977: 939).

Starting from these assumptions Hannan and Freeman define their domain of analysis by stating that (1) their analysis takes account only of one mechanism that produces isomorphism (that is, natural selection but not learning) and (2) that, unlike Hawley, their analysis takes account of the fact that each population may be in contact not only with a single environment with certain given features but with a series of multiple environments, in the sense that the environment will change over time.

Regarding the natural selection mechanism itself, Hannan and Freeman hold that "from a population ecology perspective it is the environment which optimizes" (Hannan and Freeman 1977: 939). This fascinating statement illustrates the reversal of perspective that the ecological argument implies with respect to traditional economic and organization theory. However, it can be criticized on the grounds that the process converges in selecting optimal forms of organization. Indeed, the mere fact that the environment helps to select organizational forms as well as decisionmaking processes in firms themselves does not necessarily imply that both these processes are governed by an optimizing logic. Both the firms and the environment may simply select organizational arrangements that are superior to other current arrangements at that time in that environment rather than select optimal arrangements—even assuming that these can be defined, which in many cases may not be feasible.

As Aldrich (1979) has pointed out, the population ecology of organizations is distinct both from conservative Darwinism (in which simply the strongest survives rather than the fittest) and also from a kind of rationalistic determinism, in which the best-fit form of organization survives rather than a better-fit form. As Hannan and Freeman (1977) themselves highlight elsewhere, the ecological determination of organizational structures can be seen as the outcome of a game between the firm and the environment in which the firm chooses an organizational form and the environment chooses a state that may be favorable or not to that form, giving rise to its prosperity or decline. This forms the general approach of the model that is discussed in greater detail in the following sections.

THE POPULATION ECOLOGY OF ORGANIZATIONS

Growth Model of a Single Population

Let us take a population of organizations with a given type of internal organization (let us say, a highly specialized and structured U-form). The opportunities for growth of this population in a given environment depend on "the capacity of the environment to support forms of organization and the rate at which the populations grow (or decline) when the environmental support changes" (Hannan and Freeman 1977: 941).

In the case of a single population whose size (number of firms in it) is X_1, the growth model can be expressed by the following formula:

$$\frac{dX_1}{dt} = r_1 \, X_1 \left(\frac{k_1 - X_1}{k_1} \right) \qquad \text{(Eq. 5.1)}$$

The growth rate in a population of firms with a type 1 organization form will depend on (1) the existing size of the population (the present number of firms, X_1) and (2) two parameters, k_1 and r_1. k_1 is the carrying capacity of that particular environment for that population: It is the maximum size, in equilibrium, for a population of firms with that organizational form in that environment. r_1 is the rate at which that population would grow naturally in that environment, in conditions not influenced by the environment's carrying capacity—that is, until the growth rate is not affected by resources deprivation.

Some research conducted in the population ecology perspective has estimated parameters k and r for different organizational populations in specific industries or economic sectors. For instance, Neilsen and Hannan (1977) have estimated the parameter (r) representing the speed of adjustment of the population's size to the carrying capacity of its own particular niche, along with some niche parameters that affect the niche's carrying capaicty (k) for three populations of organizations that comprise the U.S. national education system: elementary schools, high schools, and universities.[1] The three types of schools are considered to have different organizational forms because their organizational systems differ on two basic dimensions: (1) the complexity of division of work among the institution's operators and (2) the degree to which the transformation process of a unit of output is intensive and resource-consuming (the amount of resources needed to transform a student). Both these variables assume higher values moving from primary schools to universities. Estimates of parameters r and k show that complex organizations' populations with high unit costs of input transformation (such as universities) take longer to adjust to their niche-carrying capacity (that is, they proliferate more slowly). Second, the niches' carrying capacities (or the greatest size that each population can attain in its niche) of more complex organizations' populations are less sensitive to the levels of available resources—that is, maximum population size responds more loosely to changes, for example, in demand levels.

Growth Model of Several Competing Populations

Let us now assume that there are two populations of organizations, characterized by the different type 1 and type 2 organizational forms. Equation 5.1, showing the growth rate of population 1 in its niche, assumes (when there is a competing population 2) the following form:

$$\frac{dX_1}{dt} = r_1 X_1 \left(\frac{k_1 - X_1 - \alpha_{1\alpha} X_2}{k_1} \right) \qquad \text{(Eq. 5.2)}$$

where X_2 is the size of population 2, and α_{12} is the effects of the presence of population 2 on the environment's carrying capacity for population 1. An analogous expression will give dX_2/d_t, or the growth rate of population 2. These formulas show that, at the extreme, if $\alpha_{12} = \alpha_{21} = 1$ (where α_{21} is the corresponding effect of population 1 on the environment's carrying capacity for population 2), both populations will rule each other out, in the sense that they depend on the *same* resources in that environment or occupy the same niche. As the authors (Hannan and Freeman 1977: 943) say,

> The broad conclusion is that the greater the similarity of two resource-limited competitors, the less feasible is that a single environment can support both of them in equilibrium. If two populations of organizations sustained by identical environmental resources differ in some organizational characteristic, that population with the characteristic less fit to environmental contingencies will tend to be eliminated. The stable equilibrium will then contain only one population which can be said to be isomorphic to the environment.[2]

Competition between Generalist and Specialist Organizational Forms in a Dynamic Environment

This equilibrium solution presupposes that different kinds of organizations are fitted to different kinds of environment. But the issue becomes complicated if one introduces the assumption that the environment will vary in an uncertain way between states that favor different types of organization. This creates the conditions for competition among specialist populations of organizations (which maximizes efficiency in responding to a single environmental configuration) and populations of generalist organizations (which are capable of surviving in a wide variety of environmental configurations, albeit less efficiently in each of them). Referring to traditional organization theory, Hannan and Freeman trace the generalist organizational type by using two organizational dimensions: (1) the maintenance of slack resources (Cyert and March 1963; Thompson 1967), which allows adaptation to partially different demands when they arise, and (2) the variety of environmental resources on which the firm's organization is simultaneously dependent.

In order to illustrate this type of organization, which the authors define as an abstract organizational form with these features, we can link the generalist organizations to more familiar classifications of the structure and strategy of business enterprises. Generalist organizations should thus include both divisional forms and highly flexible organic or highly differentiated and integrated functional forms (Burns and Stalker 1961; Lawrence and Lorsch 1967). In agreement with the prescriptions of these structural contingencies' models, the natural selection theory leads to the conclusion that specialist organizations will beat generalist ones in a stable environment. Indeed, under stability generalist organizations will not realize the potential benefits of their greater flexibility and will incur higher costs of slack resources maintenance and nonoptimal exploitation of resources. However, where the environment is unstable, the population ecology theory extends and to some extent alters the conclusions reached by the traditional theory of structural contingencies.

In Hannan and Freeman's model for unstable environments, changes in environment pose differing demands for organizational adaptation according to at least two features of such changes: (1) the diversity or distance between possible environmental states and (2) the average length of time in which the environment remains in each state. These features of environmental volatility affect two aspects of organizational costs: (1) the cost of organizational change (restructuring or reorganization costs) and (2) the cost of error, or maladaptation if the firm does not adapt. As Hannan and Freeman (1977: 952) convincingly argue,

> The problem of ecological adaptation can be considered a game of chance in which the population chooses a strategy (specialism or generalism) and then the environment chooses an outcome (by, say, flipping a coin). If the environment "comes up" in a state favorable to the organizational form, it prospers; otherwise, it declines. However, if the variation is fine grained (durations are short), each population of organizations experiences a great many trials and environment is experienced as an average. When variation is coarse-grained, however, the period of decline stemming from a wrong choice may exceed the organizational capacity to sustain itself under unfavorable conditions.

The authors first determine which organizational forms are superior in the case of fine-grained (or short-duration) changes. Under these conditions better-fit arrangements will depend on the incompatibility of the changes undergone by the environment. If the changes are not deep-seated, a generalist arrangement will be superior, whereas if they are profound (that is, require different organizational skills and capabilities), a specialist arrangement will be superior.

In effect, where changes are slight, the cost of adapting to different states of the environment will be low because the capabilities required are similar. Where changes are marked, a generalist arrangement will incur high costs when continuously adapting to environmental states that differ substantially from each other. By contrast, a specialist arrangement will lead to costs of maladaptation throughout periods in which the environmental configuration does not suit the firm's distinctive skills. For specialist arrangements to be superior when the environment is changing between dissimilar states, it is thus vital that these changes be fine-grained so that periods of maladaptation are short.

It should be noted that because fine-grained changes are important from an organizational viewpoint, they must be uncertain—that is, different environmental states should have approximately the same likelihood of occurring. In fact, if there are some environmental states that have been proven to recur much more frequently than others, one returns to a condition approximating stability (that could be defined as a condition in which a single environmental state occurs at a frequency equal to one). This is an interpretation of the authors' assertion that the state of an environment with fine-grained variations is experienced as an average or expected state. From the viewpoint of the organization required, an environment that is predictable in the sense that it has one state more likely than others is equivalent to a stable environment in which the specialist organization will outperform others.[3] Regarding the kind of organizational arrangement that can be expected to be superior in environments where there is no uncertainty, the conclusions of the ecological perspective thus coincide with those of traditional organizational theory.

However, population ecology assertions diverge when it comes to uncertain environments. The ecological model leads to the conclusion that where the environment varies frequently between different states, a specialist organizational form that suits any one of such states will be superior to a flexible or generalist form, on the grounds that the cost of continuous adaptation will be superior to the cost of maladaptation for short periods. The conclusions of the ecological model developed by Hannan and Freeman are summarized in Table 5-1.

The polymorphic form, mentioned in the table, represents an alternative to the generalist type for coarse-grained environmental changes. It is a federation or group of several different specialist

Table 5-1.   Selected Organizational Forms by Type of Environmental Uncertainty.

Frequency of Change	Compatibility between Environmental States	Superior Organizational Forms among Several Competing Populations
Fine-grained (short duration)	Compatible (similar) environmental states	Generalist
	Incompatible (dissimilar) environmental states	Specialist
Coarse-grained (long duration)	Compatible (similar) environmental states	Generalist
	Incompatible (dissimilar) environmental states	Generalist or polymorphic

organizations. As familiar examples of polymorphic structures we can think of quasi-hierarchical, federative forms, such as holding structures, or franchising and consortia networks.

A polymorphic form has its own distinctive organization costs. In addition to the cost of adapting the firm's different activities, which requires shifting investments among different businesses, there will be the cost of running the central structure needed to coordinate several quasi-firms. Indeed, Hannan and Freeman's justification (1977: 954) for this type of organization is that "When the environment is uncertain and coarse-grained and subunits difficult to set up and tear down, the costs of maintaining the unwieldy structure imposed by federation may be more than offset by the fact that at least a portion of the amalgamated organization will do well no matter what the state of the environment."

Further Organizational Typologies: r-Strategist and k-Strategist Organizations

This basic model has been further developed by Brittain and Freeman (1980). The basic model presupposes that there are two fundamental organizational strategies (generalist and specialist) whose success in guaranteeing a population's survival depends on three environmental variables: (1) uncertainty about the combinations of resources that will be available, (2) compatibility between different resource configurations, and (3) the frequency of change between those states. However, the authors note that in ecology there is another basic distinction between survival strategies, which is generally expressed using the parameters in the population growth equation ($dx/dt = rx(k - x)/k$). The distinction is between r strategies and k strategies, and their comparative superiority depends on a further environmental dimension—the density with which a given resource space is already populated. r-strategist organizations have strategy/structure arrangements that enable them to gain first-mover advantages: "Their structure makes them relatively inexpensive to set up; that is, they concentrate on activities that require low levels of capital investment and simple structures. They are called r-strategist because they trade on speed of expansion" (Brittain and Freeman 1980: 311).

By contrast, k-strategist organizations compete in terms of efficiency, which "generally involves higher levels of investment in plant and equipment and more elaborate organizational structures." Thus "k-strategist organizations generally expand more slowly into new resource spaces than r-strategists, because the structure generating competitive efficiency frequently preclude the rapid adjustments necessary to capture first-mover advantages" (Brittain and Freeman 1980: 312).

Four kinds of basic organizational forms are defined by combining the properties of generalist and specialist organizational forms with those of the r-strategist and k-strategist types, while retaining the polymorphic arrangements as a fifth structural alternative. The properties are summarized in Table 5-2.

Brittain and Freeman (1980) discuss examples of each of these organization types in the semiconductor industry. Their review of

Table 5-2. Selected Organizational Forms and Characteristics of Industry.

Organizational Form	Dominant Competitive Advantage	Structural Properties	Characteristics of Industry
r-specialists	First-mover advantages	High specialization, low organization costs	Uncertain, fine-grained, incompatible variations. New low-density niches created by technical and product innovation.
r-generalists	First-mover advantages	Slack, structural flexibility, product differentiation	Uncertain, fine-grained compatible variations. Low-density niches as a result of entry barriers arising from learning-by-doing advantages and experience curves.
k-specialists	Efficiency	High specialization, highly structured organization	Stable, mature markets. Or marginal niches, with surpassed but still profitable technology, within dynamic industries. Or market outlets represented by one or few firms.
k-generalists	Efficiency	Diversification, highly structured organization	Uncertain, coarse-grained, compatible variation. High price competition.
Polymorphs	Ability to change niche mix	Multispecialization. Unrelated business diversification (risk reduction)	Uncertain, coarse-grained, incompatible variations.

the history of this industry leads them to extend the relationship between uncertainty in an industry and efficient organizational forms: More uncertain industries are populated not only by populations of more flexible organizations but principally by a greater variety of populations of organizations. Indeed, in uncertain and rapidly developing industries a large number of new niches are constantly opening up as a result of technical and product innovation. These coexist with existing niches that are becoming mature but are still profitable and with protected niches (such as by government or know-how barriers) with a low rate of uncertainty.[4] This variety of niches, which typically comprises an uncertain, dynamic industry, can sustain a variety of efficient organizational forms isomorphic to each niche.

Research Applications

The population ecology model has generated research at three levels.[5] A first level is organizational demography, which is aimed at constructing the general properties of population dynamics. The main data in this area relate to the births and deaths of firms.

An important area of demographic research involves analyzing the relationship between a firm's death rate and its age. The hypothesis, put forward years ago by Stinchombe (1965), is that business organizations are subject to a liability-of-newness phenomenon. Interest in this assumption has been revived in recent years as increasing attention has been devoted to the life cycle of organizations (Freeman 1982; Kimberley and Miles 1980). The existence of infant mortality in business organizations is consistent with the findings of Hannan and Freeman (1980) on organizational populations in three types of industries (restaurants, semiconductor manufacturers, and newspapers) and on populations of trade union organizations operating at the national level.[6] For business firms, not nonprofit organizations or trade unions, firm death rates fall exponentially as the years pass in all three industries. The death rate virtually reaches its asymptotic value over about fifteen years. They thus have measured how long infancy lasts in the life cycle of firms that all originate from the same organizing wave.[7] By controlling death rate variations by firm size, the authors conclude that size does not appear to affect the risk of death and that therefore liability of newness cannot be reduced to liability of smallness. In support of this hypothesis it is worth noting that the annual death rate in the United States in populations of small business organizations such as restaurants is around 10 percent, a much lower figure than is usually expected for this type of business.

The second and third levels of empirical research carried out as part of PEO involve (1) work on population dynamics in relation to niche dynamics and (2) studies on communities of competing populations that cohabit one particular industry.

For example, the study on restaurants was conducted in order to also test the hypothesis that generalist and specialist organizational forms' differential survival rates depend on the type of environmental uncertainty. Three kinds of organizational forms were investigated: generalist restaurants (with a large number of items on the menu, with service adaptable to customers' demands) and two types of specialist restaurants (fast food and ethnic restaurants). The mortality rate for both generalist and specialist forms was then related to uncertainty indicators (variability in aggregate sales in California) and the duration of incompatible environmental states, which produced significant correlations pointing in the expected direction.

VARIATION, SELECTION, AND RETENTION IN BUSINESS ORGANIZATION

Aldrich (1979) studied organizational mechanisms that can generate the three basic subprocesses of evolution—that is, variation, selection, and retention—in the context of business enterprises' organizational systems. Mechanisms that generate variations in organizational structures *among* firms are the establishment of new firms or changes in ownership. New firms may be set up with new organizational arrangements, which often continue until selection processes intervene that lead to continued survival or failure. Changes in ownership can also provide the needed push to overcome structural inertia and undergo organizational change.

Within organizations there are important sources of unplanned, spontaneous change that stimulate the emergence of organizational variations. One of these unplanned change factors is staff turnover, particularly at management level. Turnover results in organizational roles' in any given period being interpreted in a somewhat different way from previous periods. As Aldrich (1979: 39) says,

A key difference between the natural selection model and traditional theories of organizational change lies in the assignment of the source of variation. Planned variation—strategy and choice—is one source of variation, but any variation will do. Hence, the natural selection model emphasizes chance events, error, and luck. Given the rational model bias of traditional organizational and economic research, there have been few attempts to test the hypothesis that unplanned variations play an important part in change.

Some kinds of organizational structures encourage, while others may hinder, the occurrence of variations. Drawing on recent work in the indeterminist approach, Aldrich identifies loose-coupled systems as superior to other types of organizational systems in terms of their ability to produce unplanned change. Indeed, both the substantial nondefinition in relationships between different parts of the system and also the wide variety of feasible behaviors tend to encourage shifts in organizational roles. It is thus reasonable to expect that this unplanned process of structural change will take place in firms that have relatively informal, decentralized, and unintegrated organizational structures.

Aldrich argues that the difference between biological and organizational evolution regarding selection mechanisms is that organization evolution does not necessarily imply the survival and failure of individual members in a population (entire firms) but can be limited to its parts (the death and replacement of organizational units). A second peculiarity of organization evolution mechanisms is the importance of (1) selection of behavioral responses (the evaluation and change of an organizational structure), (2) selective diffusion of successful organizational variation through imitation between firms, and (3) selective retention of successful variations within firms by observing results over a period of time.

About this second feature, however, it is questionable whether it is appropriate to think of the imitation of past successful behaviors or of other firms' successful behaviors as selection mechanisms. They are decisionmaking processes that lead to individual learning of organizational solutions rather than natural selection processes. In fact, the processes of behavior selection were treated early in the theory of organizations as decisionmaking systems (March and Simon 1958; Cyert and March 1963).

Organization learning can, however, be produced by natural selection mechanisms *within* the organization itself. Both Aldrich (1979) and Weick (1979a) cite managerial selection and promotion mechanisms as a process of natural selection: Successful behaviors for the system are achieved by substituting individual managers. Here again, however, changes in corporate behavior brought about by substituting people is an alternative to the same people learning or rationally choosing new behaviors.

The population ecology theory does not provide a specific perspective on retention mechanisms operating in organizations. Formal organization by itself, with its role prescriptions and procedures, is the main retention mechanism in social evolution. As Aldrich says, at the core of most organizational theory and practice is the construction of collective memory structures that ensure the reproduction of behaviors and maintenance of selected organizational structure and processes, although they are not usually seen in this light.

THE SCOPE OF NATURAL SELECTION APPROACHES

One of the propositions advanced by Aldrich (1979) on the conditions that favor natural selection is that its effectiveness in determining feasible organizational forms is contingent on certain features of the firms in the environment. Citing the statistics on bankruptcy in U.S. firms, Aldrich notes that small businesses and firms that do not have access to government support tend to be more vulnerable to failure.

Although there is little doubt that government support acts as a protective factor—after all, state intervention is deliberately intended to alter the selection mechanism generated by market forces—it is doubtful both theoretically and empirically whether the size of a firm in itself frustrates the selection mechanism.

Taking the theoretical angle first, Freeman (1981: 1448) points out that

> A confusing problem involves limitations on the usefulness of the model. Government agencies rarely fail. Small organizations fail at a higher rate than large ones. One might quarrel with the factual bases of such assertions, but more important is the fact that one chooses a time frame and therefore the rate of failure among big organizations relative to little ones may be irrelevant. If one is doing field research, one trades off number of organizations observed against failure rate with respect to time. During any given period, fewer elephants than fruit flies die, but no biologist would argue that natural

selection processes do not affect elephants or that such a theoretical perspective should be excluded from the analysis of their evolution.

The results of Hannan and Freeman's (1980) work support the
thesis that the intensity of natural selection action is more dependent
on the age of a firm than on its size and plays a more important role
in the early stages of an organization's life cycle. Even so, it may be
observed that large firms are often coupled with market structures
characterized by small numbers, whereas, as Hannan and Freeman
(1977: 960) stress, a prerequisite for the operation "of the type of
random mechanisms that underlie population ecology models" is the
presence of large numbers of firms. Accordingly, in practical terms,
the PEO model may be much more relevant to small businesses, at
least in those cases where smallness is combined with youth or competition among large numbers of firms.

If this is so, some conditions can be defined in which one can fair-
ly confidently expect natural selection processes to operate. In the
first place, the resource space that delineates an environment must be
limited. Limited resources are a necessary condition for a maximum
size to be obtained by any one particular population of organizations
or by several competing populations.

Second, the operation of a selection mechanism implies that the
relationships between firms are governed by market forces. Environmental states must thus be subject to exogenous variables that the
firms cannot influence. Organizational forms have to be mutually
exclusive alternatives among which the environment can choose. By
contrast, if the number of firms is small enough for them to govern
and coordinate their actions by reciprocal communication and influence, thereby determining their own environmental states, then the
natural selection mechanism weakens. This means, among other
things, that the kind of industry that can be most usefully studied in
terms of natural selection will be highly fragmented industries. Indeed, according to the interorganizational relations theories discussed
in Chapters 2 and 3, the market mechanism in industries with small
numbers of firms will tend to be replaced by hierarchical structures
or by mixed forms of organizational and social coordination.

Third, natural selection is likely to play an important role in determining organizational arrangements in industries with low entry barriers that are at an early stage in their life cycles. In fact, in these
conditions there will be a high birth rate of new firms, lack of ex-

perience about better-fit organizational arrangements, a low level of slack resources available as a result of firms' setting up costs, and a high degree of environmental uncertainty intrinsic to the newness of activities. All of these conditions are conducive to a high rate of firms' infant mortality.

RATIONALITY IN NATURAL SELECTION: PEO VERSUS OTHER THEORIES

The proponents of the PEO perspective stress that natural selection is an alternative way of achieving fit organizational forms with respect to organizational adaptation by learning and decisionmaking. Organizational change is therefore an alternative to the death of individual firms with a given form of organizational structure. A further alternative, less emphasized, is that evolution in populations of organizations implies the birth of new firms as an alternative to the growth of existing firms. The ecological model is based on the premise that adaptation to a growing resource space occurs through the proliferation of firms instead of through the growth of individual firms. The reasons that one type of evolution may prevail over the other and vice versa are not explained in detail by the PEO theory. In any case, they can be worked out from the body of economic analysis on conditions that lead to market failures and then related to the PEO's domain.

Seen from a market and hierarchies perspective the occurrence of an evolutionary process in an industry by firms' proliferation rather than by individual firms' growth will depend on the configuration of production and transaction costs that prevail in that industry. If, for instance, economies of scale, learning-by-doing advantages, and the specificity of know-how are low and consequently entry barriers are low, conditions for market failure will not exist. This will favor growth in the size of the population of firms rather than growth in the size of individual firms.

Once one assumes that large-numbers conditions are present in which natural selection mechanisms can come into action, a further consideration should be the criteria, or attributes, of organizational forms that the environment will select as the best structure. In other words, if the operating rationality is that of environment, what are the preferential properties of organization structures as judged by the rationality of environments? The fundamental argument underlying PEO is that the organizational arrangements that are actually selected (that is, generalist or specialist arrangements) will depend on two factors. The first is the size of economies of specialization and scale that can be achieved by using a specialist as opposed to a generalist organizational form. The second is the trade-off between the costs of adapting a generalist organization to cope with environmental states and the cost of errors arising from periods of maladaptation in a specialist organization. It thus follows that natural selection, at least as conceived and applied to business organizations, will yield organizational forms on the basis of the economies achieved in production costs, organization costs, and change costs.

These criteria are similar to those suggested in standard models of rational choice of organizational forms, such as the organization failure framework and the structural contingency theory. Thus, the PEO theory provides considerable support for these models because it analyzes the external sanctioning mechanism that should motivate firms to adopt internal organizational forms that are efficient in terms of production and organization costs *in large-number situations.* This consistency between PEO and rational design models of organization structures cannot be extended outside the large-numbers situations, which constrain the theoretical scope of natural selection processes.[8]

In conclusion, the PEO perspective has made distinctive contributions to other current organization theories. As noted, the theoretical domain of natural selection is bounded to the determination of firms' internal organizational arrangements because the ecological proliferation-to-death process of individual firms' organizations is an alternative to the process of changing organizational boundaries. From this standpoint, the biological analogy limits the application of the natural selection model to determining mainly internal organization. Even so, the PEO theory does extend in three important ways our understanding of the contingency mechanism or the way in which the internal organization adapts to the environment.

First, the PEO perspective makes it clear that two different kinds of processes can lead to fit organizational forms' prevailing: (1) a process whereby the firm itself selects (chooses) good organizational solutions and (2) a process whereby the environment makes a selection from among firms with different organizational forms. It also provides a model of the mechanisms that govern the latter process, which had previously not been covered in organization theory.

Second, the PEO perspective has specifically applied the natural selection model to institutions pursuing profit objectives. This has enabled several general conclusions to be drawn, including that the criteria that natural selection applies to determine superior organizational forms—in competitive situations—are overall economies in organization, production, and change costs, irrespective of whether the firm has a rationally designed organizational structure.

Third, compared to the traditional structural contingency theory, PEO has also shown that the characteristics of the environment on which superior efficiency, and hence differential survival, of various organizational forms depend include not only the degree of uncertainty but also the sign of uncertain variations. Indeed, the relative superiority of any particular arrangement will also depend on whether the environment happens to be pointing in a negative or positive direction—that is, whether uncertain events (environmental states) are favorable or unfavorable.

Finally, the PEO models take into account costs derived from structure dynamics, which is a source of costs that is overlooked in the generally static perspectives of organization design. For example, both SCT and M&H hold that decentralized organizations (in which much information is processed peripherally) and flexible organizations (which can alter their configuration in line with changes in the environment) are superior where the environment is variable and uncertain. In the PEO models it has been demonstrated that this is not always the case, if account is taken of the cost of actual changes in the organization that are needed to keep abreast of changes in the environment. Taking into account change costs leads to predictions that, if the variations required are very wide, a more rigid and centralized specialist organization may again become superior to a flexible one.

These interpretations of the logic of natural selection lead to some conclusions about the basic epistemological features of the PEO model. In fact, it is often presented, by supporters and critics alike, as a perspective captive of environmental determinism that either does not take account of, or restricts, the firm's freedom of choice.

Indeed, the PEO model does specify what organizational forms have a higher degree of fitness (that is, higher probability to survive and proliferate in various types of environment), but its criterion for selecting such forms is a long way from the simple principle of environmental isomorphism. Despite its biological analogy, which may tempt critics to point in that direction, the PEO does not deserve to be accused of a crime of determinism for at least two reasons. First, it concedes that there may be several possible better-fit positions rather than a single best-fit position. Second, in the highly competitive conditions in which the model applies validly, corporate behavior is actually subject to more constraints than in other conditions and can be more easily predicted. It accordingly calls for the construction of more deterministic models.

NOTES

1. The niche parameters cover the effects on the carrying capacity (k) of changes in resources available such as fluctuations in demand (the number of possible candidates for enrollment).

2. The growth model for several populations of organizations can generally be expressed for M competing populations. Equation 5.2 will thus be redefined as the following system of M equations:

$$\frac{dX_i}{d_t} = r_i X_i (k_i - X_i - \alpha_{ij} X_j)/k_i \; i \; (i = 1, \ldots, M)$$

This defines the growth model for a community of populations of organizations, which may be seen, for example, as all the competing organizations in a given industry.

3. From a methodological standpoint, the model works out analytically what organizational forms are superior as a function of the diversity between environmental states, where the environment can fall into two states. Better-fit organizational forms are superior in terms of the degree of expected fitness (isomorphism to each environmental state weighted by the frequency of occurrence of each state).

4. However, it can be argued that the structural contingency theory, if it is not applied mechanically, is not contradicted by this conclusion. In fact, the required degree of structural flexibility does not immediately depend on uncertainty in the industry as much as on the task environment that the firm has chosen for itself within the industry—that is, its product/market niche in the population ecology sense.

5. This paragraph refers to ongoing research projects as well as completed investigations. In fact, it is a laborious task to assemble significant empirical

data in an ecological perspective because it is a process that takes long time periods and requires that very large numbers of firms be covered. Furthermore, despite the ready availability of hard data on corporate birth and death rates, the measurement of organizational arrangements often requires direct access to the firms concerned.

6. The survey on restaurants was restricted to urban areas in California and covered 1,099 establishments (a random sample of the total) from 1977 onward. The survey on newspapers covered newspaper populations in Argentina, the Irish Republic, and the United States over the past 200 years. The semiconductor industry is of much more recent origin, and most of the firms are concentrated in Silicon Valley in California: It was thus possible to code the history of some 1,000 firms between 1941 and 1975.

7. An *organizing wave*, a term coined by Stinchcombe (1965), is a period in which firms proliferate at a high rate because of the opening of new niches or new industries.

8. The natural selection argument has long been used by economists to defend their prescriptive theory of firm behavior. This tradition was started by such authoritative figures as Machlup (1946) and Friedman (1953), who defended the profit maximization hypothesis on the basis of the natural selection argument. In line with this tradition, Williamson (1981) has more recently applied this assumption to the selection of organizational forms. As has been seen, however, it is hard to justify this argument except in large-numbers situations. In less competitive conditions the firm *may* select superior forms on the basis of efficiency, but it may also enlarge the number of characteristics of the organization to which positive preferences are to be given. See Winter (1975) for a critique of the generalized use of the natural selection argument by economists.

6 THE ADAPTATION APPROACH REVISITED

Many of the phenomena analyzed in the new research perspectives discussed thus far cannot be explained or predicted as part of traditional structural contingencies theory. These phenomena can be classified into four broad categories:

1. Instead of adapting its organization to the environment, the firm may adapt the environment (that is, to a large extent other organizations) to itself. It is thus important to see what conditions in the relationship between the firm and its environment are likely to favor internal adaptation and what conditions favor a decision to change the other organizations. Both the RD and M&H perspectives have shown that the factors that condition internal adaptation as opposed to exerting external influence will center, among other things, on two main variables: the firm's degree of dependence on scarce resources (the relative substitutability of the focal firm and of its counterpart) and the degree of uncertainty.

2. It is possible that a firm may decide to adapt its organization to the environment but may in fact adapt to its own model of that environment (that is, to its own interpretation of environmental stimuli). It is also possible that adaptive action taken by a firm has an unexpected effect on the environment (such as on com-

petitors or consumers), so that the firm's final posture is one of nonadaptation because its adaptation has been to an environment that no longer exists. In both cases, the process of adaptation has been biased. In this case, conditions that can hinder or even prevent the adaptation process center on uncertainty as to the environment to which the firm is adapting. This means that the degree of uncertainty experienced by the firm has an ambiguous effect on organizational change: On the one hand it encourages and requires adaptation, but on the other hand it obstructs the process of adaptation.

3. In addition to being able to change or adapt its internal organization, a firm can also change its own boundaries. Expanding boundaries by taking over other firms or by internalizing activities is exercising influence on the environment. The size of the firm also becomes an organizational variable to be determined in relation to the state of the environment. Here, again, the features of the environment that are relevant to decisions on whether to expand (or restrict) the boundaries of the organization have been shown to center on uncertainty and dependence on scarce resources.

4. If the adaptation process does not occur in individual firms because of structural inertia, or if it occurs in a distorted fashion because of perceptual or interaction biases, the natural selection mechanism will replace the organizational learning mechanism, where there is competition for scarce resources. Again, high uncertainty about the characteristics of external demands and high pressure on resources are shown to be fundamental independent variables as to the type of organizational adaptation process that will occur.

    The recent contributions of Lawrence and Dyer (1980 and 1983), of the Harvard school has reformulated the structural contingencies theory to take into account some of these factors.

The main reform to the old SCT postulated in the new approach from the Harvard school to macro-organizational issues has been to combine the dimension of uncertainty with that of resource dependence as the environmental variables on which the best-fit organizational system for a firm will depend. In doing this, Lawrence and Dyer have sought to bring together many of the other ideas about organization developed in the 1970s.

Indeed, as shown, uncertainty and resource dependence are two necessary variables in the explanation of the comparative effectiveness of the main types of organizational forms. Aldrich (1979) has even made explicit recommendations to combine them (see Chapter 1). This is why we consider the new model here, although it does not seem to have had significant impact in the United States. There is some problem in the way in which Lawrence and Dyer have combined the two variables, by considering them to be mutually independent and sufficient to determine a single most effective and efficient organizational solution. This point will be developed in the last section of this chapter covering industrial adaptation framework. The first sections will outline the basic assumptions of the perspective and its principal propositions about the efficiency of various organizational forms in different types of environment.

BASIC ASSUMPTIONS OF THE INDUSTRIAL ADAPTATION FRAMEWORK: UNCERTAINTY, RESOURCE SCARCITY, AND EFFICIENT INNOVATION

The industrial adaptation framework is directed more toward organizational learning or design than toward natural selection models, perhaps because learning can be more easily translated into prescriptions for corporate behavior. According to this prescriptive stance, acknowledging that organizational adaptation through learning or design is not the only feasible alternative, Lawrence and Dyer seek to identify the conditions under which adaptation is the most likely response. They define the organizational adaptation as "the process by which an organization and its *chosen* domain *interact* and evolve toward more *mutually* acceptable exchanges"[1] (italics added), a process that requires the introduction of "innovations without losing existing efficiencies" (Lawrence and Dyer 1980: 7-10).

There is thus a difference between the notion of adaptation, as defined by Lawrence and Dyer, and adaptation as used in the natural selection approach. In the industrial adaptation framework (IA), *adaptation* is not synonymous with *fitness*, and not even with conscious or learned fitness. It implies environment dynamism and a continuous organization dynamics to meet its demand. Stable environments can require fit (or isomorphic) organizational structures;

in dynamic environments the best-fit, most efficient organizations are adaptive (or efficiently innovative).

Lawrence and Dyer attempt to answer the question of why some firms and some industries are more adaptive than others. They seek to pinpoint conditions that foster (1) a conscious process of adjustment on the part of the organization to environmental demands, and in particular to other organizations, and (2) the adoption of organizational arrangements that are in themselves adaptive, or flexible (that is, suited to environments that often change their configuration). In short, they take a new perspective on the old issue of conditions that encourage innovation in the firm. They are concerned with pursued, deliberate innovation that is expected to be effective and not with random, unforeseen, or unplanned processes of innovation. In this sense, the industrial adaptation perspective is complementary to the natural selection theory.

Lawrence and Dyer base their explanation of the comparative capability of firms in introducing effective innovations on this hypothesis: "Innovation has a curvilinear relation to the uncertainty of information in the focal organization's domain, conditioned by the degree of resource scarcity; and efficiency has a curvilinear relation to resource scarcity in the focal organization domain" (Lawrence and Dyer 1980: 11).

The authors restate this hypothesis by observing

> that the number of "effective innovations" (defined as innovative trials that at least passed the test of effectiveness in achieving the desired outcome) can be expected to increase in response to the stimulating effect of an increasing amount of uncertainty. . . . This positive relation between these variables continues to some limits where, because of human cognitive limits, the additional uncertainty simply acts as confusing noise and the number of effective innovations drops.

When there is heavy pressure on resources, it will likely distract attention from the innovation process. Severe resource scarcity would be likely to lower the rate of innovation because no resources would be available to seek solutions differing from those already in existence. On the other hand, under low resource scarcity there would not be enough stimuli to innovate and become more efficient. Both innovation and efficiency would thus be low with overabundant resources.

It might be proposed that if the rate of innovation falls as resources become more scarce, a high level of efficiency could be maintained beyond this point of pressure on resources. High levels of efficiency might be achieved even where resources were too scarce to permit a high degree of innovation. But Lawrence and Dyer postulate that efficiency will also begin to fall beyond a given (even though very high) degree of scarcity: "When very high resource scarcity is experienced, the firm's resource starvation will cause the neglect of

Figure 6-1. Hypothesized Relationships between (a) Uncertainty and Effective Innovation and (b) Resource Scarcity and Efficiency.

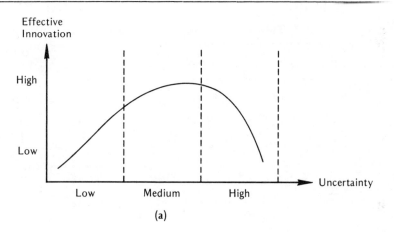

(a)

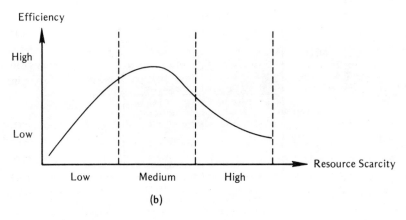

(b)

Source: Lawrence and Dyer (1980); Lawrence (1983).

machine maintenance, the preservation of adequate work-in-process inventory banks, the hiring of replacements, etc. and, thereby, the loss of efficiency in existing routine operations" (Lawrence and Dyer 1980: 12).

Summarizing, the authors postulate that the rate of effective innovation has an inverted U-curve relationship to the level of uncertainty (Figure 6-1a); that the rate of efficiency follows a similarly shaped relation to the degree of resource scarcity (Figure 6-1b); and that, in combination, intermediate levels of uncertainty and resource scarcity delineate an area in which a maximum degree of efficient adaptation is likely to be achieved (Figure 6-2).[2]

In the industrial adaptation framework, these hypotheses are applied to the more specific issue of explaining the differential rate of efficient adaptation (or innovation) in different industries. The nine areas of adaptation represented by the quadrants in Figure 6-2 each delineates an organizational environment characterized by differing levels of uncertainty and scarcity of resources that are used

Figure 6-2.   Analytical Framework of Organizational Adaptation.

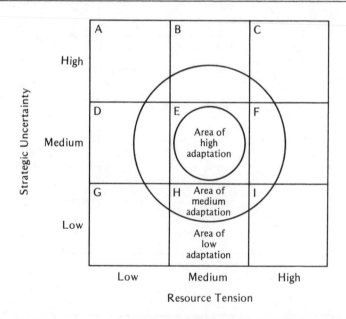

Source: Lawrence and Dyer (1980); Lawrence (1981).

to classify different industries. The two environmental dimensions described by Lawrence and Dyer are

1. *Information domain.* The variable that represents this dimension is called "strategic uncertainty." It is measured by the number of competitive variations on the offer side, by the frequency of variations in consumer preference, and by the degree in which knowledge generators and diffusors such as universities, the government, corporate R&D, industrial associations, and so forth play their stabilizing, uncertainty-reduction role.

2. *Resource domain.* The variable that represents this dimension is called "resource tension." It is measured by indicators such as the relative availability of sources of raw materials, human resources and capital, and the size of market outlets based on existing customers, competitors, and public policies.

INDUSTRIAL CONTINGENCIES

Lawrence and Dyer place different organizational forms in each of the areas of adaptation on the basis of what is known from the literature about organization types and the conditions under which they have achieved success. They draw from the work of Burns and Stalker (1961) (a study on organic organizational systems capable of generating a high rate of innovation in very dynamic industries, such as electronics); Lawrence and Lorsch (1967) (on efficient differentiation and integration as a function of industry's uncertainty); Cohen, March, and Olsen (1976) (work that led to a definition of the loosely coupled system as a possible type of surviving organization under conditions of extreme uncertainty); and Mintzberg's (1979) classification of organization structures, one of the organizational types identified by Mintzberg but not covered in other traditional literature is the professional bureaucracy—a highly specialized but non-integrated system that can survive where resources are abundant).[3]

The strategic profiles of firms in different areas are based on the work by Miles and Snow (1978) that identifies four clusters of firms with distinctive dominant strategic behaviors. These strategic approaches are (1) defenders, or firms that specialize in restricted product/market combination and are competitive largely in terms of

Figure 6-3. Location of Institutional Strategies and Organizational Forms.

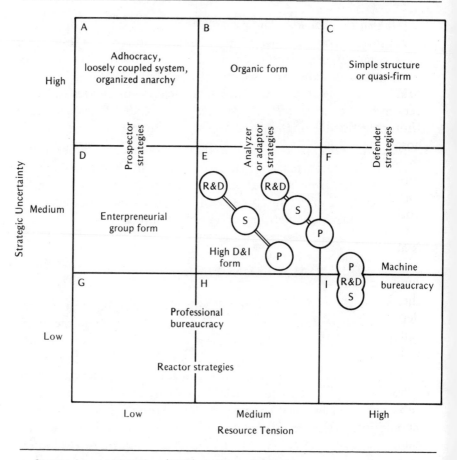

Source: Lawrence and Dyer (1980); Lawrence (1981).

internal efficiency; (2) prospectors, or flexible innovative firms that exploit new market opportunities; (3) analyzers, or firms that rationally design and adapt their organizational structures to changing environments; and (4) reactors, or firms that are poorly oriented to external influences and take corrective action only in response to a major build up in pressure from the environment.

Lawrence and Dyer associate one particular type of strategy/structure combination with each area of adaptation, as is schematically depicted in Figure 6-3. The authors then discuss examples of industries that are at stages of their life cycles that represent the various areas of adaptation. On the basis of historical analysis, these industries are described as populated by firms with the expected type of organizational structure and strategy. These are summarized below (a later section of this chapter provides a critique of the proposed location of industries and strategy/structure types within the framework):

Area A. According to Lawrence and Dyer, areas characterized by uncertainty and plentiful resources are typified (at least in the United States) by some service sectors like private universities and hospitals. A higher degree of uncertainty is usually experienced by these types of organizations than is generally the case in manufacturing industries. This is less due to the variability of external factors than to the fact that technology is not clearly understood and both preferences and goals are difficult to define.

Cohen, March, and Olsen have argued that in such conditions it is also difficult to develop a specialist hierarchical structure of subgoals and subunits. The prevailing organizational form in these types of industry will thus tend to be a loosely coupled system, the behavior of which will respond to the particular goals of departments rather than to an overall organization preference function. The firm's strategy is classified as prospective—that is, it is assumed that different organizational units will try to exploit every new opportunity encountered in their particular subenvironments.

Area D. This is the typical entry area, represented by new markets with unexploited resources but with a high degree of uncertainty. The strategy/structure combination that best fits these conditions is the small-size, innovative, *r*-strategist, or prospector organization.[4]

Area B. These are sectors that are still relatively new but are at a more advanced stage of development. They thus are densely populated and correspondingly experience higher degrees of resource tension. Typical industries in this area are semiconductors, transistors and high technology in general. In these industries, following Burns and Stalker (1961) and subsequent research in the structural contingencies paradigm, the most appropriate organizational arrangement in these conditions is the organic system—that is, a flexible, decentralized, informal, and highly integrated structure both in terms of corporate strategy and internal role system.

Area E. This is the area in which the rate of efficient innovation can reach its peak, based on the hypotheses set out in the previous paragraph. The level of uncertainty is high (the industry is dynamic), but the life cycles of both the industry and the firm within it have reached maturity. Under these conditions, innovation is to be introduced through conscious decisionmaking processes, while at the same time there is considerable motivation for innovation because resources are neither too scarce nor overabundant. The organizational form best fitted to the requirements of maximum consciousness and efficient adaptation is, in the author's view, the highly differentiated and integrated (D&I) organization. Indeed, this type of structure was identified by Lawrence and Lorsch (1967) as the most efficient structure in terms of profitability in a relatively dynamic industry such as special plastics.[5]

Areas F and I. These are mature industries but unlike area E have little opportunity for product differentiation because they manufacture commodities in a price-competitive environment. As examples, Lawrence and Dyer cite most of the mechanical engineering and the steel industries, part of the food industry, and the container industry as studied by Lawrence and Lorsch (1967). In these areas, particularly area I, the best-fit organization is a highly formal and centralized form that requires a low degree of integration because it is oriented toward high productivity and cost cutting. This organizational profile, which in organization theory is commonly termed a mechanistic system, is associated with a strategic profile that the population ecologists would define as k-specialist and that the strategy and structure paradigm would call a defender. Here the firm's competitiveness is based on its ability to procure resources in a densely populated environment and to use those resources by maximizing the input/output ratio in highly specialized manufacturing processes.

Areas G and H. Examples cited by Lawrence and Dyer are ATT, state-controlled and government-protected firms, and, for area G, public agencies and state-owned firms. The reference here is to the type of organizational bureaucracy, in its pathological version generated by means substituting ends analyzed by Merton (1949) and Selznick (1957). Crozier (1963) and Mintzberg (1979) have also analyzed such systems in terms of the internal group pressures and vested interests that they create. This arrangement prevails where there is not much uncertainty or scarcity of resources and corresponds to the professional bureaucracy as defined by Mintzberg.

Area C. The opposite pole to areas G and H in Lawrence and Dyer's framework is an area in which firms are highly dependent on external factors. These may be consumers, in markets in which there is nearly perfect competition, or single large firms that provide the only market outlet for large numbers of small, highly substitutable firms. Examples are industries in which there are barriers to firm growth (technical and otherwise) such as the restaurant industry and some retailing. It is asserted that, of all the low adaptation areas (which least favor conscious organizational change) this is the area that most favors the operation of the alternative mechanism of organizational change provided by natural selection through high failure rates.

Indeed, in this area, as in all high uncertainty areas, Lawrence and Dyer postulate that distortions in perception of the environment are particularly common. This element of friction, that affects the firm as it seeks efficient adaptive actions and structures, tends to strengthen the hand of natural selection. Second, competition among large numbers of firms and the scarcity of the resources controlled by each of them make it hard to follow alternative courses, either by taking autonomous action in seeking to influence the environment or by reducing dependence on it—for example, by turning over production lines to different products and modifying the organization accordingly. The predominant corporate strategy in this area will thus be defensive, and the firm's organization will be an elementary simple hierarchy.[6]

THE EVOLUTION OF INDUSTRIES AND ADAPTATION

The industrial adaptation framework as discussed thus far consists of a static analysis of strategy/structure combinations required in different environments where these environments that are conceived as the industries to which the firms concerned belong. Lawrence and Dyer also develop a dynamic analysis of the life cycle of industries and firms. Here they make use of contributions from the population ecology of organizations and industrial economics.

Figure 6-4. Location of Industrial Structures and Life Cycle Dynamic.

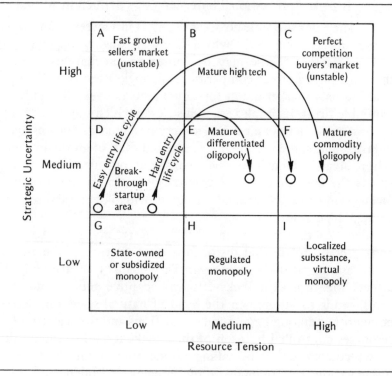

Source: Lawrence and Dyer (1980); Lawrence (1981).

They identify a typical life cycle in relation to the nine areas of adaptation, with particular reference to manufacturing industries. This is shown in Figure 6-4 along with a characterization of the areas in terms of the industrial structure they tend to represent. The areas in the upper left section of the diagram represent new, unconcentrated, rapidly growing industries. They are therefore typical entry areas, in which the life cycle of a firm begins. In ecological terms r-strategists will tend to predominate in these conditions. Their chief competitive advantage lies in their ability to grasp fresh opportunities as they arise and in terms of population to expand rapidly on the strength of the first-mover advantages they gain by occupying new niches. However, the resulting situation is unstable by nature because the growth in size of both populations of firms and of individual firms has the effect of decreasing resources in the industry, while uncertainty increases because of competitive interdependence. These conditions, typical of area B, start fostering k-type competitive strategies based on the ability to secure resources and use them efficiently in a situation where the size and number of populations of organizations start to approach the limit that can be sustained by the industry's resources.

The further development of an industry may then depend on how far its products can be differentiated. Where product differentiation is feasible, the structure of the industry may shift toward a differentiated oligopoly (area E) in which scarcity of resources and competitive uncertainty are limited by partially differentiating the resources on which different firms depend (such as different market segments). On the other hand, where there is little scope for new or further product differentiation, the industry will tend to become a competitive oligopoly based on undifferentiated goods, or commodities (area F).

This possible third stage in the life cycle of an industry corresponds to the point where resources are at their scarcest. According to Lawrence and Dyer, it may result in the appearance of a third strategic type beside the dominating K-strategist organization. This is the so-called s-strategist organization, whose main feature is a high tolerance to stress, as analyzed by ecologists in biology (Grime 1974). Firms and organizations in this category are extremely efficient at using what little resources are available, either because their niche in the environment is itself arid (the biological analogy is a desert) or because that niche has almost reached its carrying capacity. Such firms will thus inhabit marginal resource spaces, which the organizational form of the dominating population in the industry is unable to use, within industries in areas C, F, and I lying to the far right of the diagram.

Empirical research work that supports the industrial adaptation framework is primarily concerned with the dynamic analysis of adaptation. It is represented by a broad-ranging historical survey of seven major U.S. industries covering the whole of the present century to date (Lawrence and Dyer 1983), as reanalyzed and rationally reconstructed through the model's theoretical categories. This research has traced the path followed by each industry through its development and has identified some common routes. In some of the major manufacturing industries covered, such as the automobile and steel industries, a trajectory has been reproduced that is close to the theoretical curve projected on the basis of industrial life cycles hypotheses.

From the conditions assumed to be typical of infant industries (area D), these industries generally shifted to area B through growth in the size and number of firms to attain a state of differentiated oligopoly in area E. At a later stage, increasing competition and decreasing returns from product differentiation led these industries into a situation of scarcer resources, placing them in area F, the mature highly competitive oligopoly. Among the other industries covered by the survey, the telecommunications sector followed a similar path until it reached area E but then diverged into a highly concentrated pattern typical of area G.

The evolution of nonmanufacturing sectors such as hospitals, farming, and building was somewhat different. Hospitals followed a lower left to upper right course, with small charitable institutions being pressured by major technical innovation toward area E and then by government intervention and increasing task complexities toward area A. Farming and building developed on lines running within area C and its neighboring quadrants. The site-specificity characterizing investments in these industries has acted as a bar to growth in the size of firms and has led to market forces prevailing over the formation of hierarchies.[7]

In addition to its descriptive value, the analysis helps us to understand how Lawrence and Dyer's model can be applied prescriptively. Both in theory and through historical research it asserts that the positive effects of corporate efficiency and innovation attain their peak under conditions where there is moderate uncertainty and pressure on resources. The model therefore prescribes centripetal trajectories toward the high adaptation area. There are at least two possible beneficiaries of prescription. One set is firms that can select their own fields of action by seeking to enter industries or niches located in the central area of high adaptation. The second set is the economic policy authorities who can intervene to alter the availability of resources and the degree of uncertainty in various ways seeking to bring industries into area E.

Second, the model prescribes that firms in or around area E should adopt the internal organization best fit to the environmental conditions in that area—namely, the high D&I form.

The model is not as useful for the peripheral areas of adaptation, which the authors deal with in less detail than the central area E. The nature of the theories and research used to define organizational forms fit to such areas is in many cases descriptive and uneven. The only conclusion that can reliably be drawn is that the organizational forms that the authors assign to each of these areas have been demonstrated to be feasible (that is, to survive) in those environmental conditions but not to be superior to other forms. Furthermore, in none of the areas of adaptation have the authors demonstrated, either theoretically or empirically, that the organizational forms that they indicate are the *only* feasible ones. This limitation to making prescriptive use of Lawrence and Dyer's model can best be considered in the discussion of its strong and weak points that follows in the next section of this chapter.

CRITIQUE OF THE INDUSTRIAL ADAPTATION MODEL

This section identifies the theoretical scope of the industrial adaptation framework and the degree to which it has extended the original outline of the structural contingencies perspective by taking account of organizational phenomena highlighted by other lines of research. Indeed, Lawrence and Dyer appear to aim at arranging different contributions and theories in an integrated whole by tackling central issues of the current debate in organizational theory. It is therefore worth attending to the merits and demerits of such an approach.

The main tenets of the structural contingencies theory recur in the industrial adaptation perspective as special cases. For example, in this new wider perspective the proposition that mechanistic organizational systems—or, more precisely, the specialist, low D&I organizational form—will dominate in stable environments, is valid only under the condition that there is a sensible scarcity of resources. By contrast, a stable but resource-rich environment will allow organizational arrangements with a lower degree of internal efficiency to succeed, with ample scope for the pursuit of particular subobjectives.

In the same way, the proposition that efficient firms in a dynamic environment will adopt a high D&I organizational structure should be circumscribed to the condition that the firm is unescapably dependent on external resources in order to provide enough motivation for such adaptation to take place. At the same time, resources must not be so scarce as to render the cost of such change prohibitive or to prevent attention being devoted to innovation.

Lawrence and Dyer's response to organizational research in the 1970s thus provides a broader perspective of structural contingencies than the original SCT. This is mainly because the construct of environment, used to determine efficient organizational structure, is two-dimensional rather than one-dimensional. Every environmental state is characterized not only by a given degree of uncertainty but also by a positive or negative sign that expresses the relative hostility of the environment in terms of availability of resources.

Second, Lawrence and Dyer set out, in formal terms, an extension of the continuum of possible organizational forms that the rise of new perspectives has conceptually brought about. High D&I structures are recast as an intermediate form, in terms of structuring the activities and power centralization. In the professional bureaucracy (Mintzberg 1979) organizational subunits have more power vis-à-vis central authority than in the D&I form case. In the loosely coupled system (Cohen, March, and Olsen 1976; Weick 1979a) the independence of the parts is compounded and amplified by the absence of any constraints posed by horizontal specialization, integration mechanisms, or central authority. There are thus many potential applications of the industrial adaptation perspective.

Lawrence and Dyer have also sought to link their macro-organizational design framework to the micro structure and individual motivation issues. In this respect, they have focused mainly on quality of working life, based on the sociotechnical approach to job design. The authors investigate the effect that different organizational forms (macrostructures) can have on the quality of working life of individuals within the organizations concerned. On the basis of traditionally accepted hypotheses of individual motivation, Lawrence and Dyer assume that job satisfaction declines in conditions of excessive uncertainty or excessive scarcity of resources. This implies that highly unstructured organizational forms, in highly uncertain environments, cause individuals working in them to become overstressed and unsatisfied in their identity needs. By contrast, in highly structured organizations, in areas where resources are very scarce, we should find the more common phenomenon of unsatisfied security needs, and a deprivation state will prevail, involving remuneration, time available, and other personal and financial resources that form the basis of individual autonomy and power in organizations. However, Lawrence and Dyer maintain that an organization characterized by too much certainty and plentiful resources will also breed dissatisfaction or fail to optimize the positive stimuli that a work environment should present to a mature individual. The professional bureaucracies in quadrants G and H will tend to leave individuals understressed and overoriented to their own resources and power, thus failing to satisfy their need for social contact, sense of belonging, and identification with the organization. The conditions that entirely meet the individuals' needs for self-actualization and enable them to be satisfied by experiencing a feeling of competence fall within the central area of the adaptation scheme (what March and Simon (1958) would have defined as an optimal tension zone).

Lawrence and Dyer conclude at this point that high D&I organizations produce the most job satisfaction as well as the maximum corporate efficiency and innovation. Yet seen in these terms without any other contingency qualification, this statement seems an overgeneralization that is hard to demonstrate both in theoretical terms and on an empirical basis. This takes us back to the limitations of the industrial adaptation framework, whose broad domain seems to be offset by some loss of precision and falsifiability. This also explains why proponents of other lines of research have considered the industrial adaptation model to be simply a reworking of the earlier work done at Harvard rather than a theory that is sufficiently wide-ranging and accurate to integrate existing research. Indeed, Lawrence and Dyer's theoretical proposal, although attractively broad, is open to various possible objections. It has at least two fundamental flaws.

Correlation between Uncertainty and Resource Scarcity

Consider, first, quadrant C in the adaptation framework, which the authors define as an area with a high degree of uncertainty and very scarce resources. They associate a state of perfect competition with these conditions. Examples cited are the restaurant and retailing industries and in general industries where the type of service or product provided, or the need for geographical spread, limits the growth of individual firms and fosters interorganizational relations governed by market forces. Also included as typical of quadrant C are quasi-firms (small enterprises that are in fact operating units, externalized parts of a production process coordinated by a central federative structure or a dominant firm) (Eccles 1981).

142 PERSPECTIVES ON ORGANIZATION THEORY

Taken as stated this statement seems contradictory to both traditional economic theory and the economic theory of market failures. These approaches propose an opposite proposition—namely, that uncertainty is a prerequisite for the failure of market mechanisms and its replacement by hierarchical forms of coordination of economic activity.

This apparent contradiction may in part be explained by drawing distinctions between the different types of uncertainty in the different approaches. The low degree of uncertainty that characterizes markets in perfect competition is, first and foremost, uncertainty of competitive origin. A large number of small firms having a high degree of dependence on external factors will tend to cancel out uncertainty arising from unexpected moves on the part of competitors. Competitive uncertainty increases if one shifts into conditions where the number of firms is lower and they can influence each other, in contrast with Lawrence and Dyer's statements (see Chapter 3).

Uncertainty that arises from external environmental factors (such as total demand variations) may, however, be compatible with maintaining a market's mechanisms within that industry, always provided that technical barriers and resource scarcity are enough to prevent firms from forming within industry associations or integrating vertically with other firms in upstream industries (see Chapters 2 and 3).

The implications of this argument on Lawrence and Dyer's scheme is that it is much harder to correctly portray areas of adaptation in terms of *overall* uncertainty and scarcity of resources than they suggest. Indeed, it may not be feasible at all. At the very least, it will require consideration of the fact that some elements in the uncertainty variable have a nonlinear relationship with scarcity of resources and the density of firms' populations in the industry, while other elements in overall uncertainty may have no relationship or even a negative relation with resource scarcity and population density. For instance, if one follows one of the possible life cycles of an industry (let us say comparing an earlier more fragmented stage with a more mature and concentrated one), competitive uncertainty affected by increased industry concentration will increase. By contrast, uncertainty about industry characteristics is likely to decrease as an effect of knowledge accumulation on production processes, consumer behavior, raw material sources, and so on. The problem of whether it is appropriate to aggregate all these different components of uncertainty and, if so, how one should be set off against another, will then emerge with all the difficulties it poses.

One Best Way of Organizing for Each Industry?

One particularly interesting finding emerging from population ecology research as observed is that uncertain industries are characterized not only by the presence of one particular form of organization (a flexible or generalist or high D&I form) but by a variety of forms. This is chiefly because new market niches are continually opening up in uncertain industries. Therefore these environments can contain a variety of niches at different stages in their life cycles, with different degrees of uncertainty and scarcity of resources. Only if populations of firms with different organizational forms are in the same niche and hence depend on the same resources can it be said that the best-fit arrangement will spread at the expense of the others. It thus seems fair to conclude that if there is any one-to-one correspondence between areas of adaptation and better-fit organizational forms, the areas concerned will be niches and not entire industries.

Second, not only the level of uncertainty but the level of resource scarcity should also affect the variety of effective organizational forms within a resource space (industry or niche). Thus, if an industry has slack resources with respect to populations of organizations established in it, a variety of organizational responses should be possible. Indeed, in munificent environments natural selection mechanisms cannot operate. At the same time differences in corporate performance attributable to differences in organization structure should be relatively modest. In fact, results should be quite satisfactory, irrespective of a firm's internal structure, or at any rate good enough in all firms to make structure-dependent performance differences virtually negligible.

As a whole, it is more difficult to determine one particular better-fit form of organization in both uncertain industries and in rich industries or niches than it is in industries or niches that offer fewer opportunities and more hazards. If this is the case, then a variety of organizational forms should be associated with adaptation areas that have a high degree of uncertainty and/or low pressure on resources, with all these organizational systems having a property of equifinality.[8]

NOTES

1. The main reform of previous SCT notions here is the acknowledgment that the environment can be chosen and eventually changed and that structural adaptation is a reciprocal, interactive process rather than a unilateral move to fit objective environmental demands.

2. The argument on which this assumption is based originates from the theory of innovation adopted in traditional organization theory, as developed by March and Simon (1958). In that theory, as Lawrence and Dyer note, the information-processing dimension of the organization/environment relationship was not seen as split by the resource scarcity dimension. Indeed, the limited amount of resources available for search was seen as a basic determinant of a decision strategy, particularly as to how innovations in existing actions are decided. In fact, traditional innovation theory states that no action or existing plan for action will be changed until it has proved to produce satisfactory results. This prerequisite can generally be easily fulfilled where resources are overabundant and where a broad range of corporate action is producing satisfactory results. Only where the environment is more severe will the necessary stimuli to innovate be generated. However, innovation is a process associated with high costs of search and error and thus calls for the firm to maintain a sufficient level of slack resources. Accordingly, either in very severe or very rich environments, the rate of innovation will fall, other conditions being equal, as hypothesized by Lawrence and Dyer.

3. The recurring example here is the public sector firm.

4. Lawrence and Dyer specifically postulate a link between some of the strategic types proposed using a contingency approach by Miles and Snow (1978) and the strategic types used in the population ecology model.

5. The high D&I organizational form maximizes the specialization of its functional operating units in relation to their subenvironments (markets, products, technological advances) and subobjectives. At the same time, it also maximizes coordination between functional departments by applying a complex mix of integration mechanisms, ranging from programs and planning, hierarchical intervention, and lateral relationships to interfunctional groups and integrating roles (see Chapter 1).

6. For the notion of an elementary structure or simple hierarchy, see Scott (1971), Rugiadini (1979), Coda (1973), and Williamson (1970, 1975).

7. We anticipate that caution is needed about this location in the scheme of market failures and hierarchical failures factors because it may be viewed as being inaccurate.

8. See Von Bertalanffy (1968); Katz and Kahn (1966); Emery and Trist (1960) for the concept of equifinality of open systems.

7 THE METADESIGN OF ORGANIZATION

This review of current organization theories has outlined the key variables covered by and the domain of application of each perspective. The models have been analyzed with a view to comparing them and seeking links between the different approaches, many of which have been developed independently of each other. This approach can suggest how the different models can be selectively applied to the type of organization problems for which they have the most potential application.

This last chapter addresses the issue of how to select adequate tools of organization design from the viewpoint of those who have to make decisions about the organizational structures. The different decision strategies discussed in this chapter do not correspond exactly to the various lines of research that have been reviewed. Indeed, as previous chapters have shown, there are areas of overlap between current perspectives, and in many cases the same prescriptions may be derived from more than one model. At this juncture we will draw on these ideas to attempt to reconstruct the overall structure of the decision problem of the organization of the firm.

Not all the theoretical perspectives covered are concerned with the choice of organizational arrangements. It has been shown that there are at least three distinct processes through which organizational structures are selected: (1) design, or *a priori* choice based on expected costs and benefits; (2) learning, or devising an organizational structure *a posteriori* on a trial-and-error basis; and (3) natural selection, whereby organizational forms are chosen by the environment by substituting better-fit firms for less-fit firms within a population of firms with different organizational structures.

This chapter takes a decisionmaking perspective and focuses on the choice between alternative design strategies. However, in considering conditions that are likely to foster the application of one design strategy rather than another, care will be taken not to overlook those conditions in which a decision can be made *not* to redesign an organization.

This decision not to redesign may be made, in the first place, because in situations where preferences are uncertain it may be more reasonable to adopt a learning strategy than a design strategy. This case is discussed in the first section of this chapter, which reviews the question of selecting organization design choices on the basis of the firm's preference structure.

Second, when considering strategies for change, one can always decide not to change anything at all, on the grounds that change has a cost (March and Simon 1958). It may be reasonable to retain the existing organization structure, even if it is temporarily not isomorphic to its environment as outlined in the natural selection model. This will be dealt with in the second section of this chapter, which reviews the choices among strategies based on (1) changing the firm's internal organization by adapting it to its environment, (2) changing the external organization by influencing that environment, and (3) adopting no change or permitting unplanned change.

At the beginning of the 1970s the issue of macro-organizational structure design was generally represented in terms of the variables shown in Table 7–1. In other words, the main propositions of the contingency theory, held that in order to maintain efficiency (con-

Table 7-1. Structure of the Organizational Design Problem in Traditional Contingency Theory.

Independent Variables	Organization Design Strategies
Task uncertainty	Design of interunit boundaries
Tasks' interdependence	Design of interunit coordina-
Economies of scale and of	tion mechanisms
specialization	

ceived and measured as corporate profitability), one needed to move one or more internal organizational levers in response to changes in the configuration of the environmental variables. Adaptation to uncertainty, interdependence, and required specialization is achieved by modifying two main classes of organizational variables, which are partially interchangeable.

The first option is to alter the boundaries between the organization's units to minimize the aggregate costs of coordination and of production generated by the new configuration of the independent variables (Thompson 1967; Galbraith 1971). By measuring these trade-offs between the coordination costs, economies of scale, and economies of specialization, it is possible to make a rational choice of the criteria on which the units are to be specialized. For example, this allows a rational choice to be made between specialization by technical function and specialization by product.

The second type of organizational variable is represented by coordination mechanisms, which can be applied between interdependent activities that cannot be aggregated within a single unit. For instance, if the greater weight has been placed on the economies of scale and specialization advantages that can be achieved by aggregating technically similar activities (such as by keeping technical functions separate from commercial functions), the interdependence between these activities will have to be resolved by planning, communications, and joint decisionmaking mechanisms connecting the units.

The mechanisms that integrate the goals and different skills of organizational units with different specializations will allow joint processing of information, negotiation processes, and the exercise of influence of one unit on another. In the classic scheme, it is assumed that where organizational units are in a state of uncertainty, these joint decisionmaking processes will lead to efficient actions for the system as a whole on two main grounds:

1. It is assumed that in a state of uncertainty rational decisions are made by a combination of several actors with differentiated skills by a process of confrontation.

2. It is assumed that negotiated solutions between parties with conflicting objectives (as functional departments typically are) will also be efficient solutions for the system as a whole, given that the distribution of power among the units is a function of their strategic importance, or criticality, in the firm.

Moreover, this rational distribution of power will in part tend to come about automatically because those organization units that control the sources of uncertainty critical for the success of the whole firm possess a major power base for just this reason (Crozier and Friedberg 1977). Accordingly, if the boundaries between units and coordination mechanisms are defined correctly, they will tend to produce an efficient distribution of power (Williamson and Ouchi 1981).

The boundaries of the problem of the design of a firm's macrostructure have broadened in the early 1980s. In this chapter, this wider perspective is translated in terms of decisionmaking strategies and two main extensions to the traditional framework are identified. The first is the hypothesis that the decisionmaking process of determining an organization cannot be adequately represented by a choice model based solely on a profitability objective. Second, in addition to strategies aimed at changing the internal organization, there may be the alternative of modifying organizational relationships with the outside environment.

ORGANIZATION SELECTION AS A DECISIONMAKING PROCESS

This book describes the various approaches to organizations by classifying them according to each approach's assumptions about the firm's structure of preferences or objectives. The importance of these assumptions is generally recognized on the ground that designing an organization is a process of selecting alternative organizational solutions on the basis of some objective. What is less generally recognized, as applied to organization design, is that the decisionmaker's goals constitute a variable, in that the firm's preference structure may assume different configurations that generate different constraints for the decisionmaking process. Thus, a decision process need not be a deductive goal-maximizing process.

However, it can be demonstrated in general that the choice of a decisionmaking strategy is applicable or feasible under different conditions of (1) the actor's state of knowledge and (2) the preference structure of that actor (Grandori 1984).

The same is true of decisionmaking strategies to solve organizational problems. For example, information economics postulates that alternative ways of organizing the same activity may be evaluated in terms of the degree to which they reduce production and organization costs. As we have attempted to show, both the organizational failure framework and the structural contingency theory actually adopt such an approach. However, information economists recognize that the firm preference structure may vary (Marschak 1954; Radner 1972) and in some cases the consequences of these variations in goals have been developed for organizational design (Williamson 1964, 1970).

An organization in which all the members have homogeneous preferences is in fact a very special case. The only problem here is to reduce the cost of transmitting information and calculating costs versus benefits, rather than also having to combine preferences and solve conflicts. With this in mind, Marschak developed a typology of groups or collective decisionmaking systems in general that was based specifically on differences in the preference structure. Marschak called groups with uniform preferences *rational teams.* There are other kinds of groups that have a collective structure of preferences with different characteristics and that therefore *should* choose differently over organizational options. These kinds of groups are discussed below.

The Foundation

In this case, it is assumed that each actor in the group has different preferences but that it is always possible to define a collective preference ordering. Williamson (1964) used this case (see Chapter 3) and considered that the management structure of a firm can be represented as a foundation rather than as the more restrictive rational team.

In the case of organizational choices this means that various alternative organizational arrangements will be rank ordered by each manager according to his own objectives. These may take the form of firm profitability, personal wealth, departmental power, or other goals. The effect or weight of individual preferences in the group preference function will depend on the relative power wielded by each manager (see Williamson 1964; see Chapter 3).

The resource dependence perspective assumes a similar stance about the firm's preference structure (see Chapter 3). The strategies for modifying the external environment propounded in the RD perspective are based on the hypothesis that the firm as a whole is pursuing objectives that involve control over resources and that such goals are not simply a by-product of profit pursuit. However, there are some problems in that the assumption of collective preference ordering presupposes that the weights and intensity of the preferences of different actors can be compared or that they are similar enough to always arrive at a collective preference function that is a single organizational solution that is better than all the others in terms of overall utility.

The Coalition

Here it is assumed that the effects of the preferences of each actor on a common overall utility function cannot be assessed. This could be the case when the actors can be considered to be different managers, different organizational units, or different interest groups.

The idea that the firm can be seen as a coalition, or a variable array of actors with incompatible preferences, has been advanced by March (1962) and Cyert and March (1963). The only principles of rationality that a collective preference ordering has to meet in a coalition are the general principles of transitivity and Pareto-optimality.[1] These general rules of logical consistency are necessary and sufficient to guarantee that the group may be able to find, when their interests are not too divergent, efficient organizational forms or types of structure that are not inferior to any other for all actors. In any case, in such multiple incomparable objectives organizational choice problems, it may happen that the set of superior forms for all participants will either be very large or empty. In both cases, working out a single efficient solution solely by calculation either of transaction costs or of power benefits is not feasible.

The only mechanism that can lead a firm that is a coalition to a collective choice of an organizational structure is negotiation. Negotiation is different from the system of weights and balances that governs a foundation. It is a process aimed at discovering the efficient trade-offs between different actors' objectives. In a coalition these trade-offs are not codified in a procedure and the real weights of objectives and participants are not specified and known to all parties.

In negotiation participants have generally no interest in completely revealing their preferences and their true walk-away prices (Raiffa 1982), which, in the case of the negotiation of organization, can be thought of as each party's least preferred, but still acceptable, structures. Participants have also different power bases, consisting of resources controlled, strategic behaviors, dialectical skills, available alternatives to the negotiated agreement, asymmetries in information available, good interpersonal relationships, cognitive abilities in working out solutions, and legitimacy in the other side's eyes (Fisher 1983).

The distribution of participants' reservation prices and power bases is fundamental for predicting, but not sufficient for prescribing, what particular solution will be reached. The single best prescription can be that the agreed on structure should *not* be a dominated solution, moving from which one or both parties can reduce its costs without damaging the others. In the language of negotiation analysis and game theory, the recommendation to seek and try to approximate is a solution that is undominated—that is, efficient. It is not possible, however, to speak of *the* efficient boundary or structure but only of an efficient *set* or range of boundaries and structures. It is only recently that organization theory has started to analyze how strategic reasoning, interaction, and the distribution of actors' power bases lead to negotiated solutions (Bacharach and Lawler 1981; Bazerman and Lewicki 1983). This lack of basic research and theory about the cognitive processes of negotiation in organizations, which have been mainly analyzed with sociological concepts, means that negotiation-based models of organizational design have been inadequately developed. This is unchartered territory, even in newer approaches to organization theory, and needs development. Some elaborations on this point are offered in the concluding section.

The Organized Anarchy

Even weaker requirements can be posed for preference structures than for the coalition case. Preferences may simply be undefined. As the indeterminist school has provocatively and, we believe, accurately stated, the problem faced by the decisionmaker is to discover or construct his or her preferences in unknown areas where a decision has to be made. Organizational choice can easily fall into this category of problems. The main question may be to elicit the kind of unforeseeable outcomes that may be produced as a result of implemented organizational solutions and *then* to assign them positive or negative values.

The source of this uncertainty may, as was discussed in Chapter 4, be an inability to predict outcomes because their determinants are too numerous and not well enough understood. Alternatively, uncertainty about preferences may be due to lack of experience or available knowledge as to what organizational arrangements produce what types of consequence at all.

Examples of such conditions can be found in recently developed fields such as information systems. For instance, a survey of decision-making processes relating to the computerization of company information systems in various Italian firms (De Vecchi and Grandori 1983) studied the organizational decisions involved in determining the size and structuring of EDP functions based on the choice of hardware facilities and application packages and whether to carry out data processing activities inside or outside the firm. The findings show that firms at the beginning of their EDP learning curve define the boundaries of the EDP unit by trial and error, through incremental changes with respect to the existing situation. When firms are at a more mature stage in EDP experience, learning about the effects of various possible organizational arrangements allows decisionmaking models to be adopted on negotiation among several different actors geared to specific goals, such as technical reliability and memory capacity, cost reduction, EDP versus utilizators' power, dependence on suppliers, and so on.

It may thus be that situations may occur, albeit not very frequently in business organizations, in which the specific configuration of costs associated with different organizational boundaries, locations, or internal structures cannot be worked out *a priori*. For example, in the case of the EDP function, it may be that hierarchical costs associated with internalization cannot be easily predicted in advance because it is difficult to foresee the reactions and behaviors that the various actors within the firm will adopt in response.

In the two cases—of organized anarchy or a coalition—the only feasible strategies for organizational selection are organizational learning strategies, rather than organizational design strategies. However, it is not merely because a learning process can lead to feasible solutions where they are difficult to work out in advance. It is also because the distinctive benefit of trial-and-error processes is to discover solutions and hence occasionally to find *new* solutions rather than limiting oneself to considering and evaluating known organizational forms.

ORGANIZATION DESIGN DECISION TREES

Let us suppose that the need to redesign an organization arises from a requirement to respond to increasing environmental uncertainty and scarcity of resources. Further, suppose that while uncertainty and resource scarcity are both marked, neither is high enough to preclude a diagnosis of the cause-and-effect relationships between organizational alternatives and their consequences or to prevent resources being allocated to change. These are, in fact, the conditions in which organizational redesign is both important and feasible.

The organization design strategy traditionally prescribed under these conditions is to differentiate and integrate the firm's internal structure to adapt to uncertainty. Elaborations on this theme can be derived both from the traditional CT and from its expanded version as put forward in the industrial adaptation framework. This course of action is depicted as a first biforcation in the decision tree represented in Figure 7-1.

An alternative option to internal organization adaptation is to seek ways of changing external relationships that reduce uncertainty and dependence on scarce resources. In the terms of the industrial adaptation perspective (Lawrence and Dyer 1983) such strategies may be a firm changing quadrant, moving toward more southwestern quadrants. Such changes would take place not as a result of an entry in new business areas but as a result of direct action taken by the firm on the industry or niche to which it belongs, or on its transactional counterparts.

A variety of external organizational strategies aimed at altering uncertainty and dependence conditions can be derived from both the main models of interorganizational relationship design (RD and OFF). These may be classified into two main categories: (1) strategies that change the *boundaries* of individual firms and (2) strategies that create or change the *coordination mechanisms* between firms. Interdependence between firms can be governed alternatively by in-

Figure 7-1. Current Structure of the Organizational Design Problem:
A Decision Tree.

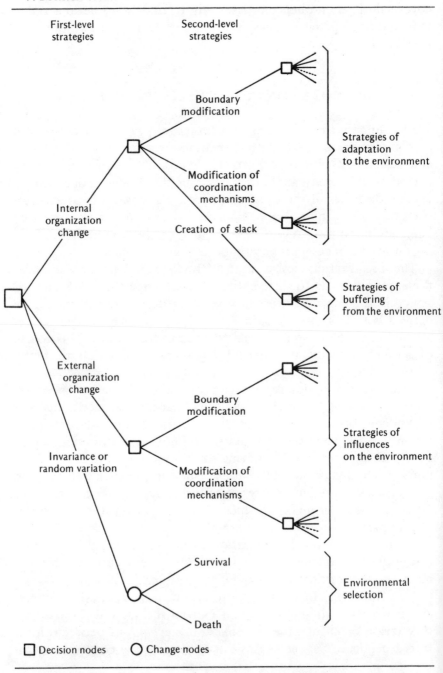

tercompany coordination mechanisms when linkages are sufficiently weak not to require integration through mergers or when it is not possible to integrate through boundaries modifications (because of constraints posed by resource scarcity or conflicting goals). The option of modifying external organizational arrangements through these two different second-level strategies, is depicted as a second biforcation of the decision tree shown in Figure 7–1.

The variables that should determine the choice of an efficient or effective organizational strategy, among those shown in this figure as second-level strategies, are delineated by the various models for internal and external organization design thus far discussed. The issue that has not been tackled explicitly is how to choose first-level organizational strategies—namely, the option between changing the internal organization as an alternative to changing the external organization; strategies both should always be evaluated against the option of maintaining the status quo. One can attempt to specify what variables should influence this choice. The various design models examined in this book provide some clues for identifying these variables, because each of them implicitly formulates some hypotheses that favor one of the three first-level strategies.

1. *Costs of organizational change.* The population ecology of organizations demonstrates the importance of assessing the expected duration of changes in environmental conditions. It may be that the costs of changing an organizational arrangement (whether internal or external) will exceed the cost of lower profits for a short period arising from an inadequate organization. Accordingly, if unfavorable environmental variations are expected to be short-term, and a major organizational change would meet the new demands, it can be cheaper to retain the existing setup.

2. *Scarcity of resources and information.* Retaining the existing organizational arrangement may be the only possible solution, even if it is not the most cost-economizing one. This is the case where there is an extreme scarcity of resources that can be allocated to the change process or there is lack of information on the environment. Further resource constraints also affect the feasibility of the first two options. Quite apart from the cost of change, strategies aimed at exercising influence on external factors usually require more resources than strategies aimed at modifying a firm's internal organization, at least when the external modifica-

tion strategies involve the extension of the firm's boundaries or interorganizational coordination mechanisms. Firms that are unilaterally dependent on external factors will encounter greater pressure toward adapting their internal organizations than those who are in a dominant position.

3. *Goals selected.* To the extent that the choice of changing the internal or external organization is unaffected by shortage of resources or information, it will depend on the firm's goals. This could occur in at least the following cases.

   a. If the sole aim is to cut overall production and organization costs, the problem can be solved by adopting a stepwise design approach: First determine the efficient boundaries and external coordination mechanisms, and once the firm's boundary is fixed, interunits boundaries and coordination mechanisms can be determined.

   b. If other goals also have to be considered, the problem will arise of how to compare the costs and benefits of changes in the internal or external organization, seen as alternative moves with respect to these goals. Let us assume, for instance, that there is a need to improve the firm's response to the market and that the firm's preferences lean toward controlling resources as one means of reducing dependence on external factors—such as in the form of a positive preference for slack resources. In this case, the option to change the external organization will become relatively more attractive than that of rationalizing the internal structure. This extends the firm's boundaries and sets up mechanisms that reduce uncertainties about the behavior of external actors who are interdependent with the focal firm. A higher valence attached to strategies of changing the external organization should also be produced where the firm's dominant goals include a reduction in dependence on internal actors with conflicting objectives, such as managers or workers' interest groups. In such cases, when a firm is seeking to reduce its internal dependence, the tendency should be to seek a reduction in the firm's boundaries within the efficient boundary. Extending organization size beyond efficient boundaries should be the tendency where the goal is to reduce dependence on external actors.

   c. If the firm's goals can be represented as being those of a coalition—namely, an array of noncomparable preferences—the relative advantages of changing the external and internal organization will alter according to the specific configuration of those preferences. Let us assume, for instance, that in assessing possible organizational changes, each unit in the organization takes account not only of profit goals but also of the effect that such changes could make on two internal power bases—that is, the amount of resources controlled by the unit and the zone of uncertainty controlled by the unit (Crozier and Friedberg 1977). Under these conditions, each unit may object to the expansion of its boundaries. This could occur, for example, where growth in size will involve internalizing sources of uncertainty over which that unit previously had exclusive control (such as acquiring major suppliers or customers, where the buying or selling function previously had sole control of the relationship).

d. Finally, the superiority of internal organizational adaptation relative to changes in interorganizational arrangements may be modified by the economic system efficiency as a whole, rather than simply by the advantages to individual firms. This is a particularly important issue because it involves a trade-off between goals for different constituent groups, all of them turning on economic efficiency.

This issue can be treated by linking it to an apparent contradiction in the industrial adaptation perspective. That model does presuppose that the best results in terms of corporate efficiency and innovation are achieved in the high-adaptation central area E. It can, however, be argued that these results may be in conflict with both a firm's power objectives (as noted also by Lawrence and Dyer) as well as its profit goals. Indeed, even if firms comply only with the principle of cutting transaction costs, it will be to the advantage of individual firms operating in conditions of high uncertainty and resource scarcity to shift toward "southwestern quadrants" rather than remaining in the central area. Thus, although conditions where industry concentration is at an intermediate stage—where uncertainty is high and where there is a major common dependence of firms on scarce resources—might be desirable for an innovation-oriented economy, they are likely to be unstable if left to the autonomous decisions of firms. This argument is consistent with the empirical data on merger and joint venture rates that reach a peak in these conditions (Pfeffer and Salancik 1978).

A conflict therefore arises between innovation and efficiency goals, on the one hand, and pure profit objectives on the other. If this is so, the Lawrence and Dyer theory that a state of high adaptation should be achieved and maintained implies substantial economic policy intervention. In some cases, such intervention is, in fact, explicitly recommended by Lawrence and Dyer in order to foster centripetal tendencies toward high adaptation areas.

This choice to include efficient innovation as a general economic system objective, even where such innovation departs from single firms' profit motives, makes the industrial adaptation perspective a more equilibrated guide than the M&H perspective to prescribing economic policy measures.

In fact, in order to draw the antitrust implications of his perspective, Williamson (1975) betrays the criterion of transaction cost reduction by prescribing public support of interorganizational arrangements that transactional economics would consider inferior. In discussing policies for highly concentrated industries, Williamson compares the dominant firm with the oligopolistic interdependence arrangements and observes (1975: 245) that

> the monopolist (or dominant firm) enjoys an advantage over oligopolists in adaptational respects since he does not have to write a contract in which future contingencies are identified and appropriate adaptation thereto are derised. . . . the monopolist can employ an adaptive, sequential decision-making procedure, which greatly economizes on bounded rationality demands without exposing himself to the risks of contractual incompleteness which face a group of conspiring oligopolists.

One would expect the author to conclude that overconcentration can be efficiency-based rather than power-based and to defend an antiregulation position. Instead, Williamson does not apply criteria such as cost reduction for the involved firms but uses consumers' benefits and the quality of output (1975: 247, italics added):

> several interdependent entities cannot realize the same degree of coordination between their policies in price and nonprice respects as can a single firm. Moreover, the price and nonprice differences that pre-

dictably arise (Kaysen and Turner 1959) will typically rebound to the consumer benefit. *Accordingly*, a *more assertive* anti-trust policy with regard to the *dissolution of dominant firms* is indicated.

This prescription runs counter to the criterion of transaction cost superiority. On the other hand, the fact that Williamson reverts to other criteria for policy prescriptions strengthens the thesis that for many purposes cost reduction is too narrow a guideline for organizational design. It is a useful analytical basis for organization decisions, but in general it is not a conclusive one.

IMPLICATIONS FOR RESEARCH ON ORGANIZATIONAL CHANGE DECISIONMAKING PROCESSES

The lines of organization thinking discussed in previous chapters suggest a number of points and propositions that can be tested empirically. However, here the discussion will focus on the empirical implications of the concluding arguments advanced in this chapter. These suggest a synthesis of the conditions in which different organizational decisionmaking strategies can be applied. In most of the literature the various approaches that have been considered thus far are seen as competing theories that offer alternative explanations of the same phenomena. To some extent they are also seen as complementary explanations of different phenomena of importance in organizations. Seen in both these ways, empirical research has an important part to play in the validation and the extension of the domains of different models (Pfeffer 1982). However, we disagree as to what are the rival hypotheses and what are the complementary hypotheses of these approaches. First, as it has been argued, some apparent rival hypotheses are instances of rival terminology (as for some M&H versus RD propositions). Second, some apparently different phenomena or different variables can be seen as the effect of different goal structures that are imposed on the organizing process.

The approach taken in this book is to identify the differences in the requirements for the application of the different approaches as different decisionmaking strategies on the organization. The central thesis of this book about the relationships between different design strategies is that the feasibility of any such strategy will depend on the firm's initial state of preferences, knowledge, and resources. This hypothesis is derived, theoretically, from the prerequisites for the applications of each approach.

The assessment of an hypothesis of this kind does, however, pose two main problems: (1) data-gathering methods and (2) correlation between organizational change decision strategy and the organization's success.

The first issue concerns procedures of enquiry through which the real preferences of the firm in organizational change processes can be discovered. One approach, which would have the advantage of minimizing distortions in the data, might be to measure the goals unobtrusively. This might be accomplished by reconstructing organization preference functions on the basis of objective indicators rather than on actors' statements. For example, following the methodologies applied in some of the approaches described here, it would be possible to correlate the outcome of organizational choices (the positioning of organizational boundaries and the coordination mechanisms used) with indicators of profitability, market power, organizational units' power, individuals' slack resources, and so forth. It may be useful to compare outcomes with random or time-dependent simulated outcomes. Such methods have the disadvantage of making subsequent interpretations of the correlations very difficult. Indeed, there are certainly a very large number of possible underlying objectives and decision processes that make it difficult to make any prescriptive use of the results.[2]

These techniques, however, might well be supported by other methods that have complementary advantages and disadvantages. For instance, process-tracing techniques that reconstruct the development of the decisionmaking process may yield a far greater body of information that could then be examined in light of unobstrusively gathered data. These tracing techniques play a fundamental part in analyzing individual decisionmaking processes and have recently been applied to the identification of organizational decisionmaking processes[3] by exploiting the more explicit traces that organizational processes leave in their wake (Anderson 1983).

The second issue is testing the relationship between the organizational change decision strategy and the organization's success. One serious complication lies in determining how success is to be measured. Indicators of short-term success, irrespective of the content of objectives, may be deceptive. As is known, a high degree of short-term profitability may lead to higher long-run costs. Short-term profitability may run counter to other short- and long-run economic and financial interests of the firm itself in addition to those of other firms or economic actors.

As an example, consider the implementation of an organizational structure that typically calls for the cooperation of more than one actor. Those preferences that had been neglected *a priori* will be brought into play *a posteriori* when the actors concerned take the opportunity to control implementation (Bardach 1977). Conversely, if a firm seeks major short-term benefits over a broad range of different goals, the losses in purely economic efficiency these entail may be untenable in the long-term. When resources are scarce enough to generate high competition, it will be the environment that dictates the long-term criteria of economic efficiency through natural selection mechanisms. Both these situations highlight the disadvantages of taking short-term success (on whatever objective) as a yardstick for corporate organizational choices. Unfortunately, they also show that long-term diverse and contradicting forces may operate so that it is hard to justify the choice of what criteria for success should prevail in the long run.

As has been observed, the economists' argument that the adoption of a principle of economic efficiency in corporate decisions, and in organizational design as a particular case, is imposed in the long term by natural selection if by nothing else has never managed to extricate itself from its surrounding difficulties (see Chapter 5, note 7). In fact, the natural selection argument has a fundamental flaw because of the very restricted conditions under which this mechanism can actually operate. As was stressed in the earlier discussion of the population ecology of organizations, the natural selection mechanism exerts an appreciable effect only in conditions where a large number of firms compete for scarce resources. This limitation is even more serious when, as in modern economic systems, competition between large-number firms thins out and small-number situations are present. Therefore, the natural selection argument becomes even weaker if it is used as conceptual support for other theories (such as the M&H theory) that prescribe organizational solutions for regulating small-number situations.

The choice to adopt a criterion of economic efficiency in organization design thus in many conditions remains a free choice and not an imperative for the firm. Even from an empirical and historical viewpoint, major examples of organizational arrangements can be found that, in the long run, have been quite successful in achieving a variety of goals that do not hinge solely on considerations of economic efficiency. Goldberg (1980) has pointed out that this interpretation applies to employment relations. There has been a general trend, throughout the world, for large trade unions to become successfully established and for labor relations to become stabilized over a long period. Hence the governance of employment relationships has tended to be hierarchical rather than market driven, independent of the nature of specific transactions.

This lends some support to the hypothesis that the goals that govern the choice of organizational arrangements may, in fact, be a variable and not a postulate. Since it is possible to design an organization on the basis of a variety of different goals and achieve success, consideration of these goals should be a subject for empirical investigation and perhaps more for descriptive rather than prescriptive research.

Some hypotheses for descriptive research on changes in corporate goals could be advanced. Regarding short-term variations, one could study the change in the mix of goals that determines the organization in relation to changes in the scarcity of resources brought about, for instance, by changed economic conditions. Or again, one could analyze cross-industry differences in the mix of goals as they relate to differing degrees of resource scarcity in each industry. The obvious hypothesis should be that the range of pursued goals narrows during unfavorable fluctuations.

Both short- and long-term analyses of the differences in the array of goals depending on the type of organizational variables to be designed would also be possible. For example, the design of a macrostructure could be more sensitive to a mix of goals that differs from the one that might govern the design of labor-relations systems and the microstructure of the organization. A reasonable hypothesis here is that where people's vital objectives are affected (as in the employment relations case) the goal-mix governing the final choice of an arrangement will be broader than in cases where there are not such strong personal effects.

Finally, some hypotheses about the long-term evolution of goals could be formed on the basis of the internal evolution laws embedded in social learning processes. For example, as some classical authors (Merton 1949) suggested, the unexpected outcomes of organizational structures, regardless of the initial objective governing its design, generate tendencies to goal proliferation. Were this idea of goals substitution and proliferation valid for all types of bureaucracies, the resulting image of a business firm's goal structure would be a self-extending goal structure that internalizes more and more objectives that were previously considered externalities. More than a modification of the configuration of the set of pursued objectives, the long-term process could be a widening of the goal structure and of a shifting toward new objectives, as the old goal structure becomes exhausted and fails to provide adequate justification for the organization's existence.

Descriptive research of this kind would be in the spirit and the approach of business history studies, and it would certainly give additional insight into the fundamental but overlooked phenomenon of preferences' formation and evolution. However, it is highly questionable that this or other kinds of research will ever allow us to prescribe preferences or at least to prescribe procedures for defining preferences. By contrast, it may well be that it will leave us with the old aphorism by Keynes, reminding that "the long run . . . is when we shall all be dead."

CONCLUSIONS

I shall now draw some conclusions from the new organization theory perspectives to suggest how their results may change one's appraisal of some important organizational forms. Only those propositions and results that are innovative and have not yet been contradicted are considered. Five points can be identified for this purpose: (1) New alternatives for organizational choice have been defined, represented by external organizational arrangements that can be seen as competing with each other and with internal arrangements; (2) among these external arrangements, intermediate forms between market and hierarchy play some particularly interesting roles; (3) the efficiency conditions of the M-form have been more clearly circumscribed, and the idea of some kind of endemic evolution toward this "stage of corporate development" (Scott 1971) has been substantially weakened; (4) new light has been thrown on efficiency properties of the "specialist form" of enterprise, so that the living space of this form appears to be wider than it was according to previous theories; (5) the revival of interest in the social bases and the functioning of economic systems has restored the importance of, and provided some efficiency rationales for, "soft," culture-based organizational systems.

The Continuum of Organizational Structures

In Figure 7-1 the decision tree of organizational design has been enriched with new branches. These new branches represent organizational alternatives that imply active intervention in other organizations. This change in the framing of organization design leads to a number of potential organizational solutions that could not have been formulated within an adaptation-to-the-environment scheme.

The classic case study in the open-system approach was the firm that developed in an expanding, easy market and that then enters a stage of turbulence because of the emergence of major competitors, the shift of strategic competitive factors from production to marketing and R&D, the shortening of product life cycles, and so on. The classic organizational solution prescribed for this problem was a

Figure 7-2. The Continuum of Organizational Forms.

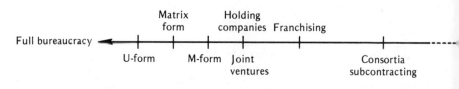

change toward a flexible, highly integrated, decentralized organizational system (Burns and Stalker 1961; Lawrence and Lorsch 1967).

A number of organizational alternatives to this solution can be defined by framing the problem as an external organization design problem rather than an internal one. The continuum of external organizing moves and the forces that should drive us to choose one of these alternatives, can be clearly expressed on the basis of some current perspectives (namely, M&H and RD).

Both internal and external organizational structures can be represented conceptually on a continuum ranging from high to low hierarchical intensity, as depicted in Figure 7-2. The two extremes are the ideal types of full bureaucracy and perfect market. Moving from centralized functional structures toward market forms, we find decentralized U-forms and the internalized market of M-form. A further step is represented by holding and joint venture structures in which property rights are still shared but bureaucracy control mechanisms are looser.

Franchising is located next because it implies no common property and is based on an exchange of services for royalties, but it is supported by usually intense bureaucratic controls. After this come interfirm agreements linking independent firms with different specializations that need intense coordination to carry out complex projects or highly interdependent activities (such as consortia for industrial and R&D projects, consortia for airports or other multiservice operations, and subcontracting in construction and engineering). The next point on the continuum is represented by formal but loose agreements such as cartels and industry associations or other horizontal agreements for limited purposes (pricing, marketing, purchasing, or EDP services). Finally, there are social modes of interfirm coordination: markets supported by integrating roles (such as interlocking directorates) and by clan relationships.

Figure 7-2. continued

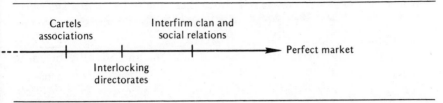

This continuum can be applied to both horizontal and vertical interorganizational relations. The independent variables, which should drive the choice of how to position on the continuum, can be summarized as follows. First, there are variables affecting transaction costs: the uncertainties to which the transaction is exposed, the specificity of investments, the measurability of performances, the degree of conflict between objectives, the number of units to be coordinated (see Chapters 2 and 3) (Williamson 1983; Ouchi 1980; Stigler 1974; Daems 1983).

Second, there are variables affecting production costs: economies of scale, specialization, and scope (Williamson 1983; Teece 1980, 1982; Eccles 1982). A more analytic discussion of how the trade-off between these costs may lead to the definition and selection of an efficient form on the continuum is addressed in the following section. In addition, in the next section we shall explore how a third class of power variables necessarily affects the choice among a *set* of efficient structures when there is asymmetric dependence between firms and conflicting preferences over organization solutions.

A Critical Role for Intermediate Forms

Pure market exchange and pure internal hierarchy are efficient forms of regulating transactions under very restrictive conditions. Perfect markets require the full transparency of price information and the full substitutability of the contracting parties. Perfect bureaucracies require performance to be measured at zero cost and activities to be fully programmable; If these conditions do not obtain, both pure institutional forms incur diseconomies.

One possible way of dealing with these diseconomies (internal and external transaction costs) is to apply the basic model developed by

Williamson (1983): The total production and transaction costs under the two systems are compared, and then the least costly system is selected. A more creative way of solving this problem is to generate intermediate or mixed solutions that are tailored to respond to cost criteria that may drive in opposite directions and thereby be more efficient.

There are many examples of this since in practice, it is unlikely that all cost parameters either point toward market or toward hierarchy. One case is the construction industry (Eccles 1982; Dioguardi 1986). In construction projects, the variability of soils and site characteristics, the complexity of the final product, and the extended time period for project completion generate high coordination needs between "work stations," both in space and time. On the other hand, there are cost criteria that favor the different specialized firms being involved, rather than by a single integrated firm carrying out the project on its own. In fact, independent firms achieve economies of specialization and scale that are specific to the type of component and equipment and to technically homogeneous subprocesses (such as heating systems, hydraulic equipment, power supply, and so forth). An intermediate organizational form such as subcontracting that simultaneously provides a high degree of interfirm differentiation and a high degree of integration (through the general contractor) is therefore generally superior in efficiency to either the market or the hierarchical alternative.

A second example is the fashion segment of the clothing industry. On the one hand, there are economies of scale and specialization that are "phase-specific rather than product-specific" (Mariotti and Cainarca 1986). These favor the vertical disintegration of the production process. Production by many small specialized firms is also favored by the high variability of demand, which increases the expected costs of a single integrated production structure. On the other hand, in ready-to-wear clothing, design, production, and assembly are closely interdependent. Usually, skilled personnel from the firm of designers directly assist the producing firms in applying specific know-how to manufacturing the final product (Perrone 1986). Although the cost of a market solution might be comparable to the cost of an integrated solution in this case as well, an intermediate form of managed market ultimately proves to be more efficient. This is exemplified in the case of most highly successful Italian fashion houses. They adopt a contracting-out system, usually based on long-established friendship, trust, and loyalty, in addition to quasi-hierarchical technical assistance and direct supervision by the design houses.

A third case is tourism. Like many other service industries it is richly populated by mixed organizational structures (Grandori 1986a). Franchising, managing contracts, preferential and exclusive contracts, and territorial district federations are common. In fact, these intermediate forms can reconcile contrasting cost requirements, such as: (1) site-specificities that link service-producing units to dispersed market outlets, and barriers to the growth of these site-specific units; (2) economies of scale in administration and common services that can be achieved by centralization; and (3) transaction costs in vertical interfirm relationships, often characterized by a marked opportunism potential (such as in the relationship between tour operators and travel agencies).

The distinctive capacity of mixed organizational forms to meet contrasting needs and requirements is particularly interesting. In effect, they can be applied not only to solve conflicts between different cost categories but also to solve conflicts between the preferences of different parties regarding organizational solutions. In other words, a negotiated approach to the design of intermediate forms can resolve one major problem left unsolved by current theories—that is, how to design an organizational structure rationally where different parties have conflicting preferences over organizational forms.

The simplest case of this is where one of the two parties in a transaction prefers an arrangement that approximates to hierarchy whereas the other prefers a quasi-market arrangement. In practice, situations of this sort are often generated by asymmetries in the relative substitutability of parties (see Chapter 2). A firm that controls unique resources and is dealing with an unsubstitutable potential partner will not see the transaction as problematic and will therefore prefer a market or quasi-market arrangement. By contrast, a firm that controls more substitutable resources and has to deal with an unsubstitutable partner will see a high potential for opportunism in the transaction and will be interested in linking with and controlling the partner as closely as possible. Other things being equal, it will therefore assign higher utility to hierarchical solutions.

For example, let us consider the case of a joint-venture formed between a leading Italian firm in vacuum technology and one of its Japanese customers that produces gas purifier equipment (Grandori and Perrone 1986). Their intention is to cooperate in production and market a highly sophisticated superpurifier, produced by combining parts of both firms' know-how. The new equipment has potential applications in the semiconductor industry, in which the Japanese firm is present. Both parties see clear advantages in cooperating, and both prefer a cooperation agreement to no agreement. However, the Italian firm controls the more sophisticated and specific know-how, whereas the Japanese firm controls the more substitutable resources of purifier production technology and of knowledge of the Japanese semiconductor market. Consequently, the Italian firm prefers a loose linkage, limited to that particular application of its product to that particular market—that is, semiconductors in Japan. The Japanese firm, however, pressures for a quasi-integration of both firms' R&D activities. Indeed, it is in the Japanese firm's interest to gain as much control as possible over the Italian firm's know-how so as to prevent other similar partnerships from being formed.

This type of negotiation over organizational arrangements could be interpreted as a distributive game.[14] The set of alternative agreements can be represented by a continuum of structures ranging from a quasi-market relationship to quasi-integration of R&D functions. The parties' preferences are exactly opposed within this set. Given the circumstances, an intermediate form (a limited joint venture) should be the expected form of agreement, in that the midpoint is the focal compromise in a purely distributive game (Raiffa 1982). The point of agreement should ideally be located closer to the Italian firm's most preferred solution, in that it has more structural negotiating power (or less substitutability) than the other.

Although a distributive game model may be perfectly adequate in modeling some negotiations about organization forms, the search for an intermediate solution may allow the parties to find some solutions that are better than others for both parties. In such cases, the negotiation structure is defined as integrative or mixed motive (Raiffa 1982; Schelling 1960). The parties can try to "widen the pie" before cutting it. First, they can seek Pareto optimal—that is, "efficient"—organizational forms;[5] then, they can choose among these efficient forms, possibly taking into account the equity in a solution that minimizes the *sum of both parties transaction and production costs.*[6]

For example, the structure of the joint-venture contract between the Japanese and Italian firms described above does, in effect, exploit some possibilities of expanding joint utility through trade-offs between factors on which the parties' preferences were complementary.

The Italian firm has a stronger preference for the exclusion of future patents and R&D activities from the joint venture. It satisfies this preference by conceding to the joint-venture exclusive control over sales of the new equipment and all other similar equipment. This protects the Japanese firm's major interest in eliminating the risk of rival partnerships (Grandori 1986b).

In conclusion, intermediate forms play a critical role in organization design because they are rich with potentially efficient solutions to at least two types of problem that would have a suboptimal or no solution within a pure market or hierarchy dichotomy: (1) organization design with multiple conflicting cost criteria and (2) organization design with multiple conflicting actors' preferences.

A Reappraisal of the Role of the M-Form

Initially it might seem that, of all hierarchical forms, the multi-divisional structure has gained in importance as a result of the contributions of recent perspectives. However, this is not a supportable conclusion. By contrast, the expected benefits of the large diversified and divisionalized firm may be more circumscribed, particularly with respect to earlier "stage of corporate development" views (Scott 1971). In these views, M-forms governing diversified activities, particularly conglomerates governing unrelated activities, are seen as more complex or better stages of organizational growth. Enterprises are supposed to evolve in an, as it were, compulsive fashion from a single product market specialization to an increasingly wide product portfolio. In the literature as well as in practice, the M-form solution has in some instances been considered as a panacea for all large businesses.

By contrast, current analyses of M-form (mainly from the M&H perspective) lead on the whole to a clear contingency view of its efficiency. In effect, although many studies have focused principally on the advantages of the M-form, the transaction-cost approach leads to both the advantages and disadvantages of the M-form being identified with respect to its functional alternative.

Its advantages include lower internal transaction costs due to managerial opportunism (discretionary behavior) and subgoal pursuit, as stressed by the M-form hypothesis. Furthermore, it involves decentralization of decisionmaking to divisions, formal and quantitative control of the divisions' final returns on performance, and quasi-price mechanisms regulating interdivisional transfers, which economize on coordination, communication, and decisionmaking costs, in comparison with the U-form's more energy-absorbing and time-consuming systems of integration.

The disadvantages of the M-form include lesser economies of scale and specialization in functional activities, as well as the cost of maladaptation to environmental demands due to neglected interdivisional (interproduct or intermarket) interdependence.

It is thus possible to draw from the M&H perspective's variables for comparing functional and divisional structures. These variables prove to be analogous to those considered in earlier contingency views (Galbraith 1971). The M-form is more efficient than the U-form (1) the higher the number and diversity of products, (2) the more their markets are uncertain, (3) the lower the economies of scale and specialization in functions, and (4) the more intense that interfunctional interdependence is with respect to interproduct interdependence.

In addition to these comparative M-form/U-form analyses, the M&H perspective extends the scope of the comparative analysis of the M-form by offering criteria for evaluating the efficiency of a diversified and divisionalized firm with respect to a market alternative. Both Chandler (forthcoming) and Teece (1980, 1982) argue that the historical and theoretical reasons for the rise of the M-form lie in its two principal properties of cost reduction with respect to independent firms carrying out the same activities.

The first efficiency rationale for multiproduct enterprise refers to production costs and is called economies of scope. Firms accumulate excess financial, physical, and human resources, generated by their initial activities. These resources could be more completely utilized if they were also applied to other activities. Firms therefore seek lateral or similar activities that, if performed jointly with existing activities, make the total costs of joint production lower than the sum of the costs of producing the two outputs separately.

Economies of scope, however, as Teece (1980) has stressed, are not a sufficient cause for the establishment of a multiproduct enterprise. In fact, it would be perfectly plausible to reduce costs by selling or contracting the use of excess resources to other firms. The second prerequisite for a multiproduct firm lies in the difficulty of transfering accumulated resources when they are transaction-specific.

This may occur with any type of resource but typically occurs when resources are represented by technical and managerial know-how. In fact, unless standardized and patented know-how is involved, the market exchange of know-how is often constrained by crucial problems (Teece 1980). First, know-how is typically connected in idiosyncratic ways with the individuals or teams who possess it (Williamson 1979). Second, there are paradoxes that prevent the exchange value of information from being defined. According to Arrow's (1971) classical statement, the fundamental paradox in this respect is that "the value of information for the purchaser is not known until he has the information, but then he has in effect acquired it without cost." Third, the learning-by-doing and transaction-specific character of managerial know-how creates by definition a market failure condition (Teece 1980). Other things being equal, the more specific that accumulated physical or human resources are (the more difficult they are to transfer or to be used by external actors),[7] the more efficient an integrated multiproduct form will be with respect to nonintegrated alternatives (such as the selling or renting of resources to independent firms). Intermediate quasi-market arrangements such as "obligational contracting" (Williamson 1979) can be efficient arrangements for know-how transfers of intermediate complexity.

The multiproduct divisionalized firm is accordingly a more efficient form of governing transactions (1) where *specific* slack resources and economies of scope are present, so that it becomes superior to market relations, and (2) when the number and complexity of the proliferating lateral activities is sufficiently high, so that it becomes superior to a functional form.

If this analysis is correct, it can be used to specify the exact conditions in which the multidivisional form is more efficient than other forms. In particular, these conditions are limited to the governance of diversification into lateral or related activities. As other studies using an M&H approach have shown, many divisional forms that are adopted in practice are excluded from these efficiency conditions. The most interesting of these other forms is the conglomerate (Williamson 1975; Teece 1982; Chandler forthcoming).[8]

The M&H perspective has therefore developed a transaction-cost-based explanation of the conglomerate firm, attributing its rise to limitations and failures in external capital markets (Williamson 1975). When financial institutions allocate capital to investment opportunities in a biased way, the internal capital market of a conglomerate may be a superior approach to recognizing opportunities and making allocations commensurate to expected returns. Nevertheless, this property of forming a substitute capital market may apply even more closely to the related activities diversification case in which the firm's distinctive competence within its sectors of activity provides a stronger reason why its corporate headquarters should be more capable of evaluating investment opportunities than the external market.

One can therefore conclude that conglomerate M-form can be— and has come to be—regarded (Chandler forthcoming) less sympathetically since the markets-and-hierarchies and visible-hand perspectives have highlighted its more limited cost-reduction properties than the related activities type of M-form.

A Reappraisal of the Role of the Specialist Form

The traditional open-system organizational paradigm does not assign a particularly attractive role to the specialized firm. It is virtually seen as a vanishing species. It is thought of as being more common in the past then in the present and better fitted to stable markets than to current turbulent environments. The mechanistic system—characterized by a high internal division of labor, low slack resources, and limited innovation capacity—is therefore seen as not being capable of operating in dynamic industries. However, this view appears to be too simplistic. Both the ecological perspective and the M&H perspective suggest that the specialist form of enterprise may have at least three roles in *dynamic* environments (in addition to its traditional life space in stable environments):

1. In industries with highly variable demand, small, phase-specialized or component-specialized firms play an important role in reducing expected production and transaction costs with respect to fully integrated enterprises. Specifically, other things being equal, vertically disintegrated production systems are efficient in conditions of variable demand when there are economies of scale and specialization in processing subphases or in the production of components. These variables help to explain, for example, the formation of large networks of smaller specialized companies

around larger generalist and flexible firms with differentiated products in dynamic industries (such as autos and plastics).

This is not to argue that long-run tendencies point toward an enlarged role for specialized firms in general. New technologies are likely to change the efficient equilibrium between internalized and externalized activities and hence between the two populations of integrated and specialized firms within an industry. For example, flexible production systems are currently generating a move toward internalization in some mechanics industry's sectors (Brandolese and Grando 1986).

2. It is not necessary for innovation processes to be generated by organic organizations capable of changing their programs of action. New business ideas can be realized by new firms, which can compete because of low set-up costs (less structural inertia and change costs), low error costs, and first-mover advantages. One example is highly specialized companies created in high technology sectors to exploit specific know-how that cannot be efficiently applied by large companies (because its efficient scale of production is too low or the markets for its application too narrow). Another instance is that of firms that provide sophisticated services that can be most efficiently produced by highly specialized firms.

In the former case the specialist form of enterprise captures the advantages and bears the risks of opening up new niches; in the latter case it is the best-fitted occupant of niches where the scale required is too low and/or the specialization required is too high for a generalist form.

3. Finally, the population ecology of organizations has demonstrated that the specialist form of enterprise is superior to the generalist form in cases where demand varies with high frequency between very dissimilar states (see Chapter 5). In both stable environments and very variable environments with short expected periods of hostility the specialist form benefits from the advantages of having no internal change costs. This type of specialist form may be found in those industries in which demand is subject to strong seasonal fluctuations or is tightly dependent on random specified variables such as the weather or on specified fluctuating exogenous variables such as income levels, as is the case with tourism and high-quality food and beverages.

A Reevaluation of the Role of
Culture-Based Systems

The notion that all economic structures include a social contract has a long history (Weber 1922; Gouldner 1960). It has also been said that the purely social mechanism of control is an alternative to rational-legal rules and utilitarian free exchange in the regulation of human behavior (Dahl and Lindblom 1953; Etzioni 1965). What new ideas have been generated by the new organizational perspectives on social control?

The organizational forms defined as clans and as loosely coupled systems can be considered together. They are similar because they are both "soft" systems based on cultures rather than structures. The major distinctive property of both is their capacity to regulate ambiguous activities and nonmeasurable performance (Ouchi 1980; Cohen, March, and Olsen 1976). These two systems differ in the conflict resolution modes they employ and hence in their objective structure. Clans cultivate clear overall objectives and invest in the socialization, homogeneization, and identification of members with respect to them (typical business examples in Italy are work cooperatives supported by political parties). By contrast, loosely coupled systems accept objectives as being undefined or ambiguous. In the case of universities and nonprofit institutions, the organizational system works through mechanisms such as the quasi-resolution of conflict (Cyert and March 1963), the incremental composition of diverging forces and interests (Lindblom 1959, 1977), and, at its extreme, where not even the actors' preferences are defined, through almost random matches among actors and behaviors (March and Shapira 1982).

Although this may not be a common perception, the novelty of these analyses from the social psychology of organization is that they do offer an efficiency rationale for the existence and spread of such systems, which may be defined as culture-based systems. This approach is very clear and explicit in the justification of clans, conceived as a more efficient form for regulating vague and long-lasting transactions (Barney and Ouchi 1983).

In the case of loosely coupled systems, one should note that both March and Weick have clearly linked these systems to conditions of ambiguity. Yet, most interestingly, one can also perceive a normative spirit in the teleology of innovation that pervades March and Weick's writings. A normative key for interpreting loosely coupled systems is that they are the only type of system that is suitable for innovative enterprises that are most uncertain in their ends and most conflictual in their effects, such as scientific research, industrial research, the arts, and allocation of public resources.

It is no coincidence that future research is being geared to collective learning processes. The analysis of loosely coupled systems can improve our capacity to construct and live in more open, experiment-oriented, and self-correcting organizations, as Campbell (1969) and Weick (1979b) have advocated. And in this context, self-correction has the very broad and liberal meaning that it has in scientific epistemology; it requires societies that are willing to learn and change not only their means but also their ends.

NOTES

1. The Pareto-optimality principle requires that for every pair of alternatives A, A', if A is preferred to A' by every member of the group, then the group will prefer A to A'. The transitivity principle requires that if a group preference ordering exists—but there is no guarantee that it emerges—it is transitive (that is, if A is preferred to A', and A' to A'', then A is preferred to A'') (Marschak 1954; Williamson 1964).

2. This is a difficulty that has already been encountered in research aimed at testing hypotheses that organizational behavior is dependent on given goals. Examples include the work of Teece (1981b) on the hypothesis of behavior aimed at maximizing profits in the M-form and research on the influence of power and efficiency goals on budget decisions in universities (Pfeffer and Salancik 1974a, 1974b).

3. A recent state-of-the-art review of this field has been provided by Hayes (1982).

4. Distributive negotiation involves a division of resources in which a gain for one party always corresponds to a loss for the other. It is a constant sum game: There are no points of agreement in which *both* parties can improve their positions.

5. Pareto-optimal, efficient, or undominated solutions are defined as all those solutions with respect to which no other solution is better for both parties or for one party without the other party's losing out.

6. This is one possible way to solve an integrative bargaining problem (Raiffa 1982). Other procedures have been developed in game theory. The point here is not to explore these procedures in detail but only to affirm that

178 PERSPECTIVES ON ORGANIZATION THEORY

organization design with conflicting interests can be addressed as a bargaining problem.

7. Resources do in fact have to be transaction-specific; they cannot be so specialized that their efficient application to other similar activities is prevented or that economies of scope cannot arise.

8. A conglomerate is a firm diversified into multiple *unrelated* businesses. Its mechanisms of control are consequently very loose and predominantly financial.

REFERENCES

Argyris, Chris, and Donald A. Schön. 1978. *Organizational Learning: A Theory of Action Perspective*. Reading, Mass.: Addison Wesley.

Alchian, Armen A., and Harold Demsetz. 1972. "Production, Information Costs, and Economic Organization." *American Economic Review* 62: 777-95.

Aldrich, Howard E. 1979. *Organizations and Environments*. Englewood Cliffs, N.J.: Prentice Hall.

Anderson, Paul A. 1983. "Decision Making by Objection and the Cuban Missile Crises." *Administrative Science Quarterly* 28: 165-83.

Anderson, Erin, and Barton A. Weitz. 1983. "Make or Buy Decisions: A Framework for Analysing Vertical Integration Issues in Marketing." Working paper, Wharton School, University of Pennsylvania.

Armour, Henry O., and David J. Teece. 1978. "Organizational Structure and Economic Performance: A Test of the Multidivisional Hypothesis." *Bell Journal of Economics* 9: 106-22.

Arrow, Kenneth J. 1951. *Social Choice and Individual Values*. New York: Wiley.

_____. 1971. *Essays in the Theory of Risk Bearing*. Chicago: Markham.

_____. 1974. *The Limits of Organizations*. New York: Norton.

Axelrod, Robert. 1973. "Schema Theory: An Information Processing Model of Perception and Cognition." *American Political Science Review* 67: 1248-66.

_____, ed. 1976. *Structure of Decision: The Cognitive Maps of Political Elites*. Princeton, N.J.: Princeton University Press.

_____. 1984. *The Evolution of Cooperation*. New York: Basic Books.

Bacharach, Samuel B., and Edward J. Lawler. 1981. *Bargaining*. San Francisco: Jossey Bass.

180   PERSPECTIVES ON ORGANIZATION THEORY

Bardach, Eugene. 1977. *The Implementation Game*. Cambridge, Mass.: MIT Press.

Barney, Jay B., and William G. Ouchi. 1983. "Information Cost and Organizational Governance." Unpublished manuscript, University of California at Los Angeles.

Bator, F.M. 1958. "The Anatomy of Market Failure." *Quarterly Journal of Economics* 72: 351-79.

Bauer, Michael, and Elie Cohen. 1983. "The Invisibility of Power in Economics: Beyond Markets and Hierarchies." In *Power, Efficiency and Institutions*, edited by A. Francis, J. Turk, and P. Willman, pp. 81-104. London: Heinemann.

Bazerman, Max H. 1985. *Judgment in Managerial Decision Making*. New York: Wiley.

Bazerman, Max H., and Roy J. Lewicki. 1983. *Negotiation in Organizations*. Beverly Hills, Calif.: Sage.

Bem, D.J. 1967. "Self-Perception: The Dependent Variable of Human Performance." *Organizational Behavior and Human Performance* 2: 105-21.

Berger, Peter, and Thomas Luckmann. 1966. *The Social Construction of Reality*. Harmondsworth: Penguin Books.

Blau, Peter M. 1964. *Exchange and Power in Social Life*. New York: Wiley.

Boulding, Kenneth E. 1968. "The Economics of Knowledge and the Knowledge of Economics." *American Economic Review* 58: 1-13.

Bower, Joseph L. 1970. *Managing the Resource Allocation Process*. Homewood, Ill.: Irwin.

Brandolese, Armando, and Alberto Grando. 1986. "Le opportunità e i vincoli per la deverticalizzazione derivanti dalle nuove tecnologie." In *Le aziende senza confini*, edited by Atti Convegno. Milan: SDA Bocconi.

Brittain, Jack W., and John H. Freeman. 1980. "Organizational Proliferation and Density Dependent Selection." In *Organizational Life Cycle*, edited by J.R. Kimberly and R.H. Miles, pp. 291-338. San Francisco: Jossey Bass.

Burns, Tom, and G.M. Stalker. 1961. *The Management of Innovation*. London: Tavistock.

Burton, Richard M., and Børge Obel. 1980. "A Computer Simulation Test of the M-form Hypothesis." *Administrative Science Quarterly* 25: 457-66.

Butler, Richard J., and M.G. Carney. 1983. "Managing Markets: Implications for the Make-Buy Decision." *Journal of Management Studies* 20: 213-31.

Cable, John, and Peter Steer. 1978. "Internal Organization and Profit: An Empirical Analysis of Large U.K. Companies." *Journal of Industrial Economics* 27: 13-30.

Campbell, Donald T. 1960. "Blind Variation and Selective Retention in Creative Thought as in Other Knowledge Processes." *Psychological Review* 67: 380-400.

_____. 1969. "Reforms as Experiments." *American Psychologist* 24: 409-29.

_____. 1970. "Natural Selection as an Epistemological Model." In *A Handbook of Method in Cultural Anthropology*, edited by R. Naroll and R. Cohen, pp. 51-85. Garden City, N.Y.: Natural History Press.

_____. 1974. "Evolutionary Epistemology." In *The Philosophy of Karl Popper*, edited by P.A. Schilpp, vol. 14-I, pp. 413-63. LaSalle, Ill.: Open Court.

Chandler, Alfred D. 1962. *Strategy and Structure*. Cambridge, Mass.: MIT Press.

_____. 1977. *The Visible Hand*. Cambridge, Mass.: Harvard University Press.

_____. 1981. "Historical Determinants of Managerial Hierarchies: A Response to Perrow." In *Perspectives on Organization Design and Behavior*, edited by A.H. Van de Ven and W.F. Joyce, pp. 391-402. New York: Wiley.

_____. Forthcoming. *Scale and Scope: The Dynamics of Industrial Enterprise 1880-1940*.

Child, John. 1982. "Organizational Structure, Environment and Performance: The Role of Strategic Choice." *Sociology* 6: 1-22.

Coase, Ronald H. 1937. "The Nature of the Firm." *Economica N.S.* 4: 396-405.

Coda, Vittorio. 1973. *Progettazione delle Strutture Organizzative*. Milan: Franco Angeli.

Cohen, Michael D., James J. March, and Johan P. Olsen. 1972. "A Garbage Can Model of Organizational Choice." *Administrative Science Quarterly* 17: 1-25.

_____. 1976. *Ambiguity and Choice in Organizations*. Bergen: Universitetforlaget.

Commons, John R. 1934. *Institutional Economics*. Madison: University of Wisconsin Press.

Crozier, Michel. 1963. *Le phénomène burocratique*. Paris: Editions due Seuil.

Crozier, Michel, and Erhard Friedberg. 1977. *L'acteur et le système*. Paris: Editions due Seuil.

Cyert, Richard M., and James J. March. 1963. *A Behavioral Theory of the Firm*. Englewood Cliffs, N.J.: Prentice Hall.

Daems, Herman. 1983. "The Determinants of the Hierarchical Organization of Industry." In *Power, Efficiency and Institutions*, edited by A. Francis, J. Turk, and P. Willman, pp. 35-53. London: Heinemann.

Dahl, Robert A. 1957. "The Concept of Power." *Behavioral Science* 2: 201-15.

Dahl, Robert A., and Charles E. Lindblom. 1953. *Politics, Economics, and Welfare*. London: Harper & Row.

De Vecchi, Claudio, and Anna Grandori. 1983. *I processi decisionali d'impresa*. Milan: Giuffrè.

Dioguardi, Gianfranco. 1986. *L'impresa nell'era del computer*. Milan: Ed. Sole 24 Ore.

Donaldson, Lex, John Child, and Howard E. Aldrich. 1975. "The Aston Findings on Centralizations: Further Discussion." *Administrative Science Quarterly* 20: 453-60.

Downey, H. Kirk, Don Hellriegel, and John W. Slocum, Jr. 1975. "Environmental Uncertainty: The Construct and Its Application." *Administrative Science Quarterly* 20: 613–29.

Duncan, Robert, and Andrew Weiss. 1979. "Organizational Learning: Implications for Organizational Design." *Research in Organizational Behavior* 1: 75–123.

Durkheim, Emile. 1893. *La division du travail social.* Paris: Alcan.

Eccles, Robert G. 1982. "The Quasi-Firm in the Construction Industry." *Journal of Economic Behavior and Organization* 2: 335–57.

Einhorn, Hillel J. 1982. "Learning from Experience and Suboptimal Rules in Decision Making." In *Judgment Uncertainty: Heuristics and Biases*, edited by D. Kahneman, P. Slovic, and A. Tversky, pp. 268–83. Cambridge: Cambridge University Press.

Einhorn, Hillel J., and Robin J. Hogarth. 1978. "Confidence in Judgment: Of the Illusion of Validity." *Psychological Review* 85: 395–416.

_____. 1982. "Behavioral Decision Theory: Processes of Judgment and Choice." In *Decision Making*, edited by G.R. Ungson and D.N. Braunstein, pp. 15–41. Boston: Kent.

Emerson, Richard M. 1962. "Power-Dependence Relations." *American Sociological Review* 27: 31–40.

Emery, F.E., and E.L. Trist. 1960. "Socio-Technical Systems." In *Management Science Models and Techniques*, edited by C.W. Churchman and M. Verhulst, pp. 82–97. Elmsford, N.Y.: Pergamon Press.

Etzioni, Amitai. 1965. "Organizational Control Structure." In *Handbook of Organizations*, edited by J.G. March, pp. 650–77. New York: Rand McNally.

Evan, William. 1966. "The Organization-Set: Toward a Theory of Inter-Organizational Relations." In *Approaches to Organizational Design*, edited by J.D. Thompson, pp. 175–290. Pittsburgh, Penn.: University of Pittsburgh Press.

Feyerabend, Paul K. 1975. *Against Method.* London: Verso.

Fisher, Roger. 1983. "Negotiating Power." *American Behavioral Scientist* 27: 149–66.

Francis, Arthur. 1983. "Markets and Hierarchies: Efficiency or Domination?" In *Power, Efficiency and Institutions*, edited by A. Francis, J. Turk, and P. Willman, pp. 105–16. London: Heinemann.

Freeman, John. 1981. "Organizations and Environments. By H.E. Aldrich." *American Journal of Sociology* 86: 1447–50.

_____. 1982. "Organizational Life Cycles and Natural Selection Processes." *Research in Organizational Behavior* 4: 1–32.

Friedman, Milton. 1953. "The Methodology of Positive Economics." In *Essays in Positive Economics*, edited by M. Friedman, pp. 3–43. Chicago: University of Chicago Press.

Galbraith, Jay R. 1970. "Environmental and Technological Determinants of Organizational Design." In *Studies in Organizational Design*, edited by P. Lawrence and J. Lorsch, pp. 113–39. Homewood, Ill.: Irwin.

_____. 1971. "Matrix Organization Design." *Business Horizons* 14 (February): 29–40.

_____. 1973. *Designing Complex Organizations.* Reading, Mass.: Addison Wesley.

_____. 1974. "Organizational Design: An Information Processing View." *Interfaces* 4: 28–36.

_____. 1977. *Organization Design.* Reading, Mass.: Addison Wesley.

Galbraith, John Kenneth. 1952. *American Capitalism: The Concept of Countervailing Power.* Boston: Houghton Mifflin.

Goffmann, Erving. 1969. *Strategic Interaction.* Philadelphia: University of Pennsylvania Press.

Goldberg, Victor P. 1980. "Bridges over Contested Terrain: Exploring the Radical Account of the Employment Relationship." *Journal of Economic Behavior Organization* 1: 249–74.

Gombrich, E.H. 1960. *Art and Illusion.* Princeton, N.J.: Princeton University Press.

Gort, M. 1962. *Diversification and Integration in American Industry.* Princeton, N.J.: Princeton University Press.

Gouldner, Alwin. 1960. "The Norm of Reciprocity: A Preliminary Statement." *American Sociological Review* 25: 161–79.

Grandori, Anna. 1984. "A Prescriptive Contingency View of Organizational Decision Making." *Administrative Science Quarterly* 29: 192–208.

_____. 1986a. "Piccole imprese, grandi corporations e networks nel settore turistico." In *Sistemi informativi per il turismo,* edited by Atti Convegno. Milan: IBM Italia.

_____. 1986b. "Multiple Objectives Organization Design." Working paper. Milan: Università Bocconi.

Grandori, Anna, and Vincenzo Perrone. 1986. "La joint-venture SIV-SUNYO." Case study. Milan: Università Bocconi.

Grime, J.P. 1974. "Vegetation Class by Reference to Strategies." *Nature* 250 (7): 26–30.

Hannan, Michael H., and John Freeman. 1977. "The Population Ecology of Organizations." *American Journal of Sociology* 82: 929–64.

_____. 1980. "Selection and Competition in the Life Cycles of Organizations." Working paper, Stanford University.

Hayes, John R. 1982. "Issues in Protocol Analysis." In *Decision Making,* edited by G.R. Ungson and D.N. Braunstein, pp. 61–77. Boston: Kent.

Hickson, D.J., C.R. Hinings, C.A. Lee, R.E. Schneck, and J.M. Pennings. 1971. "A Strategic Contingencies Theory of Intraorganizational Power." *Administrative Science Quarterly* 16: 216–29.

Hinings, C.R., D.J. Hickson, J.M. Pennings, and R. Schneck. 1974. "Structural Conditions of Intraorganizational Power." *Administrative Science Quarterly* 19: 22–43.

Hawley, Amos H. 1950. *Human Ecology: A Theory of Community Structure.* New York: Ronald Press.

_____. 1968. "Human Ecology." *International Encyclopedia of the Social Sciences*, pp. 328-37. New York: Macmillan.

Hayek, Friederich A. 1945. "The Use of Knowledge in Society." *American Economic Review* 35: 519-30.

Hedberg, Bo L.T., Paul C. Nystrom, and William H. Starbuck. 1976. "Camping on Seesaws: Prescriptions for a Self-Designing Organization." *Administrative Science Quarterly* 21: 41-65.

Hirschman, Albert O., and Charles E. Lindblom. 1962. "Economic Development, Research and Development, Policy Making: Some Converging Views." *Behavioral Science* 7: 211-22.

Horwicz, M. 1956. "Psychological Needs as a Function of Social Environment." In *The State of Social Science*, edited by L.D. White. Chicago: University of Chicago Press.

Katz, Daniel, and Robert Kahn. 1966. *The Social Psychology of Organizations.* New York: Wiley.

Kelley, H.H., and A.J. Stahelski. 1970. "Social Interaction Basis of Cooperators' and Competitors' Beliefs about Others." *Journal of Personality and Social Psychology* 16: 66-91.

Kimberly, John R., and Robert H. Miles. 1980. *The Organizational Life Cycle.* San Francisco: Jossey Bass.

Kotter, J., and P. Lawrence. 1974. *Mayors in Action: Five Approaches to Urban Governance.* New York: Wiley.

Kuhn, Thomas S. 1962. *The Structure of Scientific Revolutions.* Chicago: University of Chicago Press.

Jacobs, David. 1974. "Dependency and Vulnerability: An Exchange Approach to the Control of Organizations." *Administrative Science Quarterly* 19: 45-59.

Jones, S.R.H. 1982. "The Organization of Work." *Journal of Economic Behavior and Organizations* 3: 117-37.

Lakatos, Imre. 1970. "Falsification and the Methodology of Scientific Research Programmes." In *Criticism and the Growth of Knowledge*, edited by I. Lakatos and A. Musgrave. Cambridge: Cambridge University Press.

Lane, M., R. Beddows, and P. Lawrence. 1981. *Managing Large Research and Development Programs.* Albany: State University of New York Press.

Lanzetta, John T., and Vera T. Kanareff. 1962. "Information Cost, Amount of Payoff, and Level of Aspiration as Determinants of Information Seeking in Decision Making." *Behavioral Science* 7: 459-73.

Lawrence, Paul. 1981. "Organization and Environment Perspective." In *Perspectives on Organization Design and Behavior*, edited by A.H. Van de Ven and W.F. Joyce, pp. 311-37. New York: Wiley-Interscience.

Lawrence, Paul, and Davis Dyer. 1980. "Toward a Theory of Organizational and Industrial Adaptation." Working paper, Harvard Business School.

_____. 1983. *Renewing American Industry*. New York: Free Press.

Lawrence, Paul, and Jay Lorsch. 1967. *Organization and Environment*. Boston: Harvard Business School.

Leontief, Wassily. 1966. *Input-Output Economics*. Oxford: Oxford University Press.

Levinthal, D., and J.G. March. 1981. "A Model of Adaptive Organizational Search." *Journal of Economic Behavior and Organization* 2: 307-33.

Lindblom, Charles. 1959. "The Science of Muddling Through." *Public Administration Review* 19: 59-88.

_____. 1977. *Politics and Markets*. New York: Basic Books.

Lipset, Seymur M., Martin A. Trow, and James S. Coleman. 1956. *Union Democracy*. New York: Free Press.

Lorsch, J., and S. Allen. 1973. *Managing Diversity and Interdependence: An Organizational Study of Multidivisional Firms*. Boston: Harvard Business School.

Lorsch, J., and J. Morse. 1974. *Organizations and Their Members: A Contingency Approach*. New York: Harper & Row.

Lowin, A., and J.R. Craig. "The Influence of Level of Performance on Managerial Style: An Experimental Object Lesson in the Ambiguity of Correlational Data." *Organizational Behavior and Human Performance* 3: 440-58.

Machlup, Fritz. 1946. "Marginal Analysis and Empirical Research." *American Economic Review* 36: 519-54.

March, James G. 1962. "The Business Firm as a Political Coalition." *Journal of Politics* 24: 662-78.

_____, ed. 1965. *Handbook of Organizations*. New York: Rand McNally.

_____. 1978. "Bounded Rationality, Ambiguity and the Engineering of Choice." *Bell Journal of Economics* 9: 587-607.

March, James C., and James G. March. 1977. "Almost Random Careers: The Wisconsin School Superintendency." *Administrative Science Quarterly* 22: 377-408.

_____. 1978. "Performance Sampling in Social Matches." *Administrative Science Quarterly* 23: 434-53.

March, James G., and Zur Shapira. 1982. "Behavioral Decision Theory and Organizational Theory." In *Decision Making*, edited by G.R. Ungson and D.N. Braunstein, pp. 92-115. Boston: Kent.

March, James G., and Herbert A. Simon. 1958. *Organizations*. New York: Wiley.

Mariotti, Sergio, and Gian Carlo Cainarca. 1986. "The Evolution of Transaction Governance in the Textile-Clothing Industry." *Journal of Economic Behavior and Organization* 7: 351-74.

Marschak, Jacob. 1954. "Towards an Economic Theory of Organization and Information." In *Decision Processes*, edited by R.M. Thrall, C.H. Coombs, and R.L. Davis, pp. 187-220. New York: Wiley.

_____. 1955. "Elements for a Theory of Teams." *Management Science* 1: 127-37.

_____. 1965. "Economic Theories of Organization." In *Handbook of Organizations*, edited by J.G. March, pp. 423–50. New York: Rand McNally.

_____. 1972. "Computation in Organizations: Comparison of Price Mechanism and Other Adjustment Processes." In *Decisions and Organizations*, edited by G.B. McGuire and R. Radner, pp. 237–82. Amsterdam-London: North Holland.

Marschak, Jacob, and Roy Radner. 1972. *Economic Theory of Teams*. New Haven: Yale University Press.

Merton, Robert K. 1949. *Social Theory and Social Structure*. New York: Free Press.

Miles, Raymond, and Charles C. Snow. 1978. *Organizational Strategy: Structure and Processes*. New York: McGraw-Hill.

Mindlin, Sergio, and Howard E. Aldrich. 1975. "Interorganizational Dependence: A Review of the Concept and a Reexamination of the Findings of the Aston Group." *Administrative Science Quarterly* 20: 382–92.

Mintzberg, Henry. 1979. *The Structuring of Organizations*. Englewood Cliffs, N.J.: Prentice-Hall.

Mohr, L.B. 1971. "Organizational Technology and Organizational Structure." *Administrative Science Quarterly* 16: 444–59.

Moore, Gwen. 1979. "The Structure of a National Elite Network." *American Sociological Review* 44: 673–92.

Nacamulli, Raul C.D., and Andrea Rugiadini. 1985. *Organizzazione e mercato*. Bologna: Il Mulino.

Neisser, Ulrich. 1976. *Cognition and Reality*. San Francisco: Freeman.

Nielsen, Francois, and Michael T. Hannan. 1977. "The Expansion of National Educational Systems: Test of a Population Ecology Model." *American Sociological Review* 42: 479–90.

Osofsky, J.D. 1971. "Children's Influence upon Parental Behavior: An Attempt to Define the Relationships with the Use of Laboratory Tasks." *Genetic Psychology Monographs* 83: 147–69.

Ouchi, William G. 1979. "A Conceptual Framework for the Design of Organizational Control Mechanisms." *Management Science* 25: 833–48.

_____. 1980. "Markets, Bureaucracies, and Clans." *Administrative Science Quarterly* 25: 129–41.

_____. 1981. *Theory Z*. Reading, Mass.: Addison Wesley.

Ouchi, William G., and Alfred M. Jaeger. 1978. "Type Z Organization: Stability in the Midst of Mobility." *Academy of Management Review* 3: 559–69.

Payne, J.W. 1976. "Task Complexity and Contingent Processing in Decision Making: An Information Search and Protocol Analysis." *Organizational Behavior and Human Performance* 16: 366–87.

Pennings, Johannes M. 1975. "The Relevance of the Structural Contingency Model for Organizational Effectiveness." *Administrative Science Quarterly* 20: 393–410.

Perrone, Vincenzo. 1986. "Davide Lorenzi, stilista." In *Casi di organizzazione,* edited by M. Decastri. Milan: Angeli.

Perrow, C. 1967. "A Framework for the Comparative Analysis of Organizations." *American Sociology Review* 32: 194-208.

———. 1972. *Complex Organizations.* Glenview, Ill.: Scott Foresman.

———. 1981. "Markets, Hierarchies and Hegemony." In *Perspectives on Organization Design and Behavior,* edited by A.H. Van de Ven and W.F. Joyce, pp. 371-86. New York: Wiley.

Pettigrew, John F. 1973. *The Politics of Organizational Decision Making.* London: Tavistock.

Pfeffer, Jeffrey. 1972. "Merger as a Response to Organizational Interdependence." *Administrative Science Quarterly* 17: 382-94.

———. 1981. *Power in Organizations.* Marshfield, Mass.: Pitman.

———. 1982. *Organizations and Organization Theory.* Marshfield, Mass.: Pitman.

Pfeffer, Jeffrey, and Gerald R. Salancik. 1974a. "Organizational Decision Making as a Political Process: The Case of a University." *Administrative Science Quarterly* 19: 135-51.

———. 1974b. "The Bases and the Use of Power in Organizational Decision Making: The Case of a University." *Administrative Science Quarterly* 19: 242-54.

———. 1978. *The External Control of Organizations: A Resource Dependence Perspective.* New York: Harper & Row.

Phillips, Almarin. 1960. "A Theory of Interfirm Organization." *Quarterly Journal of Economics* 74: 602-13.

Pugh, Derek S. 1976. "The 'Aston' Approach to the Study of Organizations." In *European Contributions to Organization Theory,* edited by G. Hofstede, M.S. Kassem, pp. 62-78. Assen NL: Van Gorcum.

Pugh, D.S., D.J. Hickson, C.R. Hinigs, and C. Turner. 1969a. "The Context of Organizational Structures." *Administrative Science Quarterly* 14: 91-114.

———. 1969b. "An Empirical Taxonomy of Structures of Work Organizations." *Administrative Science Quarterly* 14: 115-26.

Radner, Roy. 1972. "Normative Theories of Organizations." In *Decisions and Organizations,* edited by C.B. McGuire and R. Radner, pp. 117-88. Amsterdam-London: North Holland.

Raiffa, Howard. 1982. *The Art and Science of Negotiation.* Cambridge, Mass.: Harvard University Press.

Ross, Lee, and Craig A. Anderson. 1982. "Shortcomings in the Attribution Process: On the Origins and Maintenance of Erroneous Social Assessments." In *Judgment under Uncertainty: Heuristics and Biases,* pp. 129-52. Cambridge: Cambridge University Press.

Rubin, Paul H. 1978. "The Theory of the Firm and the Structure of the Franchise Contract." *Journal of Law and Economics* 21 (April): 223-33.

Rugiadini, Andrea. 1979. *Organizzazione d'impresa.* Milan: Giuffrè.

_____. 1983. "Evoluzione e prospettive dell'organizzazione aziendale." In *L'organizzazione nell'economia aziendale*, pp. 1–21. Milan: Giuffrè, Convegno dell'Accademia Italiana di Economia Aziendale.

Schelling, Thomas C. 1960. *Strategy of Conflict*. Cambridge, Mass.: Harvard University Press.

Scott, Bruce R. 1971. *Stages of Corporate Development*. Boston: Harvard Business School.

Selznick, Philip. 1949. *TVA and the Grass Roots*. Berkeley: University of California Press.

_____. 1957. *Leadership in Administration*. New York: Harper & Row.

Simon, Herbert A. 1945. *Administrataive Behavior*. New York: Macmillan.

_____. 1957. "A Behavioral Model of Rational Choice." In *Models of Man*, edited by H. A. Simon, pp. 241–60. New York: Wiley.

_____. 1969. *The Sciences of the Artificial*. Cambridge, Mass.: MIT Press.

Staw, Barry M. 1980. "Rationality and Justification in Organizational Life." *Research in Organizational Behavior* 2: 45–80.

Stern, L. W., and W. M. Morgenroth. 1968. "Concentration, Mutually Recognized Interdependence and the Allocation of Marketing Resources." *Journal of Business* 41: 56–67.

Stigler, George J. 1964. "A Theory of Oligopoly." *Journal of Political Economy* 72: 44–61.

_____. 1974. "Free-Riders and Collective Action: An Appendix to Theories of Economic Regulation." *Bell Journal of Economics and Management Science* 5: 359–65.

Stinchombe, Arthur L. 1965. "Social Structure and Organizations." In *Handbook of Organizations*, edited by J. G. March, pp. 142–93. New York: Rand McNally.

Teece, David J. 1980. "Economies of Scope and the Scope of Enterprise." *Journal of Economic Behavior and Organizations* 1: 223–47.

_____. 1981a. "The Multinational Enterprise: Market Failure and Market Power Considerations." *Sloan Management Review* 22: 3–17.

_____. 1981b. "Internal Organization and Economic Performance: An Empirical Analysis of the Profitability of Principal Firms." *Journal of Industrial Economics* 30: 1–27.

_____. 1982. "Toward an Economic Theory of the Multiproduct Firm." *Journal of Economic Behavior and Organizations* 3: 39–63.

Thompson, James D. 1967. *Organizations in Action*. New York: McGraw-Hill.

Tosi, Henry, Ramon Aldag, and Ronald Storey. 1973. "On the Measurement of the Environment: An Assessment of the Lawrence and Lorsch Environment Uncertainty Scale." *Administrative Science Quarterly* 18: 27–36.

Tversky, Amos, and Daniel Kahneman. 1971. "The Belief in the Law of Small Numbers." *Psychological Bulletin* 76: 105–10.

_____. 1982. "Causal Schemas in Judgments under Uncertainty." In *Judgment under Uncertainty: Heuristics and Biases*, edited by D. Kahneman, P. Slovic, and A. Tversky, pp. 117-28. Cambridge: Cambridge University Press.

Van de Ven, Andrew H., and William F. Joyce, eds. 1981. *Perspectives on Organization Design and Behavior.* New York: Wiley.

Von Bertalanffy, L. 1968. *General Systems Theory.* New York: Braziller.

Weber, Max. 1922. *Wirtschaft und Gesellschaft.* Tübingen: Mohr.

Weick, Karl E. 1976. "Educational Organizations as Loosely Coupled Systems." *Administrative Science Quarterly* 21: 1-19.

_____. 1979a. *The Social Psychology of Organizing.* Reading, Mass.: Addison Wesley.

_____. 1979b. "Cognitive Processes in Organizations." *Research in Organizational Behavior* 1: 41-74.

Whitt, Allen J. 1980. "Can Capitalists Organize Themselves?" In *Power Structure Research*, edited by G.W. Domhoff, pp. 97-113. Beverly Hills, Calif.: Sage.

Williamson, Oliver E. 1964. *The Economics of Discretionary Behavior: Managerial Objectives in a Theory of the Firm.* Englewood Cliffs, N.J.: Prentice-Hall.

_____. 1970. *Corporate Control and Business Behavior.* Englewood Cliffs, N.J.: Prentice-Hall.

_____. 1975. *Markets and Hierarchies.* New York: Free Press.

_____. 1979. "Transaction Costs Economics: The Governance of Contractual Relations." *Journal of Law and Economics* 22: 233-61.

_____. 1983. "Technology and the Organization of Work." *Journal of Economic Behavior and Organizations* 4: 57-62.

Williamson, Oliver E., and William G. Ouchi. 1981. "The Markets and Hierarchies Program of Research: Origins, Implications and Prospects." In *Perspectives on Organization Design and Behavior*, edited by A. H. Van de Ven and W.F. Joyce, pp. 347-70. New York: Wiley.

Winter, Sidney. 1971. "Satisficing, Selection, and the Innovating Remnant." *Quarterly Journal of Economics* 85: 237-61.

_____. 1975. "Optimization and Evolution in the Theory of the Firm." In *Adaptive Economic Models*, edited by R.H. Day and T. Groves, pp. 73-118. San Diego: Academic Press.

Yuchtman, E., and S.E. Seashore. 1967. "A System Resource Approach to Organizational Effectiveness." *American Sociology Review* 32: 891-903.

Zan Stefano. 1982. *La cooperazione in Italia.* Bari: De Donato.

NAME INDEX

Alchian, Armen A., 46, 49
Aldag, Ramon, 9, 22 n. 2
Aldrich, Howard E., xix, 17–18, 19
21, 23 n. 6, 72, 106, 116, 117, 118,
127
Anderson, Craig A., 83
Anderson, Eric, 37, 52 n. 9
Anderson, Paul A., 160
Argyris, Chris, 84
Armour, Henry O., 39, 43
Arrow, Kenneth J., 57, 62, 173
Axelrod, Robert, 53 n. 14, 83

Bacharach, Samuel B., 151
Bardach, Eugene, 161
Barney, Jay B., 44, 47, 49, 52 n. 9,
69, 176
Bator, F.M., 52 n. 5
Bauer, Michael, 50
Bazerman, Max H., 99, 151
Beddows, R., 1
Bem, D.J., 85
Berger, Peter, 7
Blau, Peter M., 5, 59
Boulding, Kenneth E., 43
Bower, Joseph L., 12, 44
Brandolese, Armando, 175
Brittain, Jack W., 105, 106, 113
Burns, Tom, 94, 101 n. 5, 109, 131,
133, 166

Burton, Richard M., 39, 43, 52 n. 9
Butler, Richard J., 45, 47

Cable, John, 43
Cainarca, Gian Carlo, 168
Campbell, Donald T., 23 n. 7, 99,
101 n. 9, 177
Carney, M.G., 45, 47
Chandler, Alfred D., 41, 43, 48, 49,
52 n. 9, 53 n. 11, 172, 174
Child, John, 8, 23 n. 6, 73
Coase, Ronald H., 32
Coda, Vittorio, 9, 144 n. 6
Cohen, Elie, 50
Cohen, Michael D., 10, 16, 82, 85, 88,
90, 91, 92, 93, 94, 100 n. 1, 131,
133, 140, 176
Coleman, James S., 45
Commons, John R., 32
Craig, J.R., 85
Crozier, Michel, 5, 9, 12, 20, 50, 59,
73, 134, 148, 157
Cyert, Richard M., 9, 10, 58, 60, 73,
82, 109, 117, 150, 176

Daems, Herman, 49, 68, 167
Dahl, Robert A., 12, 176
Demsetz, Harold, 46, 49
De Vecchi, Claudio, 152
Dioguardi, Gianfranco, 168

191

SUBJECT INDEX

Joint ventures, and interorganizational relations, 17

Knowledge
organizational learning and, 83-86
uncertainty and, 14

Learning process, *see* Organizational learning
Life cycle of organizations, 115-116; *see also* Natural selection argument

Managers
discretionary behavior theory for, 55, 56-58
organizational failures with multiple objectives and, 56
staff turnover and, 116-117
Markets
clan forms applied to, 47
hierarchical form and efficiency in, 38-39
information requirements and conflict resolution properties of, 45
transaction cost regulation through, 37
Markets and hierarchies (M&H) approach, 25, 29-51
basic assumptions in, 29-32
criticisms of, 36-38
discretionary behavior and, 75-76
efficient boundaries and, 32-38
diversification and, 75
interdependence and, 32-33
interfirm organization and, 18-20
interunit boundaries and transaction costs and, 33
market failure and, 30
opportunism and, 31-32
power and, 50-51, 73-77
resource specificity and, 34-36
small-numbers condition and, 31, 36
technological transformations of, 49
transaction costs and, 36-37
uncertainty and, 29-31
vertical integration and, 74-75
Mergers
horizontal integration and, 64
interdependence and, 62-63

interorganizational relations and, 17
vertical integration and, 63-64
M-form hypothesis
reappraisal of role of, 171-174
transaction costs and, 40-44
Multiple objectives, 55-77
managerial discretionary behavior theory and, 55, 56-58
organizational failures with, 56-58

Natural selection argument, 103-123
basic assumptions of, 104-107
competition between generalist and specialist organizational forms in, 109-112
conditions for, 119-120
economic sectors and market niches and, 105-106
government support and, 118-119
organizational learning and, 99-100
population ecology of organizations (PEO) and, 103-104, 107-116
rationality in, 120-123
research applications of, 115-116
r-strategist and k-strategist organizations and, 113-115
scope of, 118-120
structural contingency theory (STC) and, 20-22
structural inertia phenomenon and, 20-21
variation, selection, and retention and, 116-118
Negotiation, and organizational selection, 150-151

Organizational costs, and structure, 26-27
Organizational learning
basic assumptions in, 83-87
garbage can model of organizational choice and, 88-94
interaction and, 86-87
knowledge processes and, 83-86
natural selection mechanism and, 99-100
random organizational processes and limits of, 97-100
structural contingency theory (STC) and, 7

ABOUT THE AUTHOR

Anna Grandori is an associate professor of business administration in Italy and holds appointments at Bocconi University and School of Business in Milan and at the University of Udine. Professor Grandori received her laurea degree in economics from Bocconi University in Milan, and, is a member of the Center for Research on Business Organizations at Bocconi. Her current research interests are decision and negotiation processes and service organizations. She has published articles in *Administrative Science Quarterly* and *Studi Organizzativi* and books on the hospitality industry (*L'impresa alberghiera*, 1983, coauthored with S. Vicari, D. Salvioni, and S. Paci), organizational decision process (*I processi decisionali d'impresa*, 1983, coauthored with C. De Vecchi), and organizational simulations (*Simulazioni di organizzazione*).